The Latin Letters of C. S. Lewis

Other Works of Interest from St. Augustine's Press

Robert Hugh Benson, *Lord of the World*

Josef Pieper, *The Concept of Sin*

Josef Pieper, *Death and Immortality*

Josef Pieper, *Enthusiasm and Divine Madness: On the Platonic
    Dialogue* Phaedrus

Josef Pieper, *Happiness and Contemplation*

Josef Pieper, *In Tune with the World: A Theory of Festivity*

Josef Pieper, *Scholasticism: Personalities and Problems of Medieval
    Philosophy*

Josef Pieper, *The Silence of St. Thomas: Three Essays*

Josef Pieper, *The Silence of Goethe*

Josef Pieper, *Tradition: Concept and Claim*

Josef Pieper, *The Chrisitan Idea of Man*

Josef Pieper, *The Platonic Myths*

Josef Pieper, *Tradition as Challenge*

Josef Pieper, *What Does "Academic" Mean?*

Josef Pieper, *Don't Worry about Socrates: Three Plays for Television*

Josef Pieper and Heinz Kastop, *What Catholics Believe*

James V. Schall, *The Regensburg Lecture*

James V. Schall, *The Modern Age*

Edward Feser, *The Last Superstition: A Refutation of the New
    Atheism*

Servais Pinckaers, O.P., *Morality: The Catholic View*

Peter Kreeft, *The Philosophy of Jesus*

Peter Kreeft, *Jesus-Shock*

Pierre Manent, *Seeing Things Politically*

Pierre Manent, *Beyond Radical Secularism*

Rémi Brague, *Eccentric Culture: A History of Western Civilization*

Rémi Brague, *On the God of the Christians*

Rémi Brague, *The Legitimacy of the Human*

Dietrich von Hildebrand, *The Nature of Love*

Raïssa Maritain, *We Have Been Friends Together* and *Adventures in
    Grace*

Albert Camus, *Christian Metaphysics and Newoplatonism*

The Latin Letters of
C. S. Lewis

C. S. Lewis

✠

Don Giovanni Calabria

Translated and edited by Martin Moynihan

Introduction by Mark A. Noll

ST. AUGUSTINE'S PRESS
South Bend, Indiana

Manufactured in the United States of America.

2 3 4 5 6 7   21 20 19 18 17 16

Library of Congress Cataloging in Publication Data
Lewis, C. S. (Clive Staples), 1898–1963.
[Correspondence. English]
The Latin Letters of C. S. Lewis: C. S. Lewis and Don Giovanni
Calabria / translated and edited by Martin Moynihan.
p. cm.
Originally published: Letters. Ann Arbor, Mich.:
Servant Books, 1988.
Includes bibliographical references and index.
English and Latin
ISBN 1-890318-34-5 (cloth: alk. paper)
1. Lewis, C. S. (Clive Staples), 1898–1963 Correspondence.
2. Anglicans – England – Correspondence. 3. Authors, English –
20th century – Correspondence. 4. Calabria, Giovanni,
1873–1954 – Correspondence. 5. Catholic Church – Italy –
Clergy – Biography. I. Calabria, Giovanni, 1873–1954.
II. Moynihan, Martin. III. Title.
BX5199.L53A4 1998
283'.092 – dc21   98-18477

The original paperbound edition (ISBN: 978-1-58731-455-1) was
published in 2009, then updated in 2016 (ISBN: 978-1-58731-457-5).

∞ *The paper used in this publication meets the minimum requirements of
the American National Standard for Information Sciences – Permanence
of Paper for Printed Materials, ANSI Z39.48-1984.*

ST. AUGUSTINE'S PRESS
www.staugustine.net

CONTENTS

FOREWORD

The Latin letters of C. S. Lewis significantly enrich what can be known about the mature years of the English-speaking world's most effective public advocate for Christian faith in the mid-twentieth century. When considered for more than their intrinsic biographical value, however, the letters also illuminate the extraordinary revolution in intra-Christian relationships that has occurred since the day in 1947 when out of the blue in Oxford Lewis received a letter, composed in Latin, from a Catholic priest of Verona. The priest, Don Giovanni Calabria, who had read an Italian translation of *The Screwtape Letters* wanted to thank the author for this work, but also to enlist Lewis for a cause that had become his life's vocation: the return "dissidentium fratrum . . . ad unitatem Corporis Christi, quod est Ecclesia" (of the dissenting brethren . . . to the unity of the Body of Christ, which is the Church).

The Introduction that follows, as well as the full notes at the book's conclusion, ably explain the circumstances that led to these letters. They also supply necessary biographical details about Father Calabria, the institution he created to care for the children of Verona, and the Italian priest's passionate dedication to the cause of Christian unity. This apparatus also helpfully explains where the letters came in C. S. Lewis' biography, stretching from the first exchange in September 1947 to Lewis' final letter in April 1961, which was the last of seven that he wrote to a colleague of Father Calabria after Don Giovanni died in December 1954. Yet it may be worth pausing, now deep into the twenty-first century, to note what the letters reveal about this famous author.

For most of us contemporary readers, the most extraordinary thing will simply be Lewis' ability, at age fifty and beyond, to compose fluent prose in Latin—sometimes at length and often with considerable conceptual complexity—after not having been called upon to do so for probably more than three decades. If we also consider the one time Lewis wrote in Italian (Letter 21), we are given a hint about his unusual capacity for languages that, not incidentally, made him such a valuable companion for J. R. R. Tolkien, another scholar of extraordinary linguistic creativity.

Yet the letters also convey much else. They show, for example, Lewis' remarkable facility in quoting from (or perhaps digging out) apposite quotations from the Vulgate Bible. His ingenuity was especially on display when he made up Latin expressions that might have astounded Livy, Cicero, or Tacitus (e.g., "dactylographica machina" for typewriter, Letter 13). There are also hints concerning how his life-long attention to Latin may have honed the always bracing clarity of his English prose. As an example, on 10 September 1949 Lewis wrote that, after a spell of fever had left him non compos mentis, he could grasp more fully what Dante had once written about the mind in relation to the person. After supplying the appropriate quotation (from Dante's Italian), what Lewis wrote in Latin—"*Operatio* mentis adest, *opus* abest"—exhibits the same lapidary concision, precise wordplay, and unmistakable clarity so often found in his English prose (The *working* of the mind is there, but not its *work*).

However much the letters communicate about Lewis as a writer, they reveal even more about Lewis as a Christian. We witness him trying out ideas about petitionary prayer that he later fleshed out in an address to a local Oxford society and even further in the posthumously published *Letters to Malcolm: Chiefly on Prayer* (Letter 22). He explained how mental assent to the doctrine of forgiven sin became an existential reality (Letter 16). And he opened his heart about the happiness that Joy Davidman brought into his life, as also his profound sorry when she passed away (Letters 31, 33, 34)

Yet for all that the letters do to deepen Lewis' biography, they contribute even more, at least by implication, to the modern history of intra-ecclesiastical fellowship. In the fall of 1947, Don Calabria expressed to Lewis his great anxiety concerning "the almost universal conflagration of war-madness," the "many boundaries . . . overthrown," and "the world . . . like a field ploughed up with so many troubles and sufferings." At the same time, the Italian priest also thought he could observe "a great aspiration of all peoples toward reform." From that last observation, he went on to hope that the day had come when the warring parties within Christendom could admit their respective failings, pray with each other, cooperate together on mutually beneficial enterprises, and move toward the reunion anticipated in Christ's prayer from John 17, "ut omnes unum sint" (that they all may be one) (Letter 1).

Lewis responded in kind. But, characteristically, his letters brought to bear a sharp analytical perspective on the barriers standing in the way of Christian unity. Thus, when drawing on personal knowledge of the land of his birth, he noted that Northern Ireland's surd cultural antagonism against anything papal mirrored the same sentiment against anything Protestant in Spain (Letter 17). He also drew on wisdom gained from his literary study to push back gently against Don Calabria's unequivocal assertion that the cause of schism was sin. Lewis reported to the priest that he had just finished comprehensive reading of the thousands of pages of vitriol that Thomas Moore and William Tyndale exchanged in their all-out ecclesiastical combat during the early years of the English Reformation. Lewis had undertaken this reading to prepare for the luminous treatment he would accord both authors in his contribution to the *Oxford History of English Literature*.[1] That specialized study

[1] See C. S. Lewis, *English Literature in the Sixteenth Century Excluding Drama* (Oxford: Oxford University Press, 1954), 165–81 (More), 181–92, 205–7 (Tyndale), and 192 (for a hint in this book of what he explained at length in his Latin letter about viewing these fierce antagonists as in some fashion joined together in spite of themselves).

gave Lewis keen insight into the character of the two historical figures, but therefore also on the great difficulty that precisely Christian *integrity* posed to Christian union: "Both of them seem to me most saintly men and to have loved God with their whole heart: I am not worthy to undo the shoes of either of them. Nevertheless they disagree and . . . . their disagreement seems to me to spring not from their vices nor from their ignorance but rather from their virtues and the depths of their faith, so that the more they were at their best the more they were at variance." Lewis' conclusion rose from ecclesiology to theology proper: "I believe the judgment of God on their dissension is more profoundly hidden than it appears to you to be: for His Judgments are indeed an abyss" (Letter 5).

* * * * *

On the broader canvass against which these letters began flying back and forth between Verona and Oxford, it is striking that almost no one in the Christian world was speaking about Christian unity with the passion of Don Calabria or the profound insight of C. S. Lewis.[2] A few contemporary statements can put their unusual correspondence into context.

In 1945, the American Protestant preacher Carl McIntyre, who stood closer to the mainstream than he would later as a fiery fundamentalist, expressed an antagonism that was by no means uncommon: "As we enter the post-war world, without any doubt the greatest enemy of freedom and liberty that the world has to face today is the Roman Catholic system. Yes, we have Communism in Russia and all that is involved there, but if one had to choose between the two . . . one would be much better off in a communistic society than in a Roman Catholic Fascist set-up." Three years later,

[2] The quotations that follow are taken from Mark A. Noll and Carolyn Nystrom, *Is the Reformation Over? An Evangelical Assessment of Contemporary Roman Catholicism* (Grand Rapids: Baker Books, 2005)

in calmer tones: "the difference between Protestantism and Roman Catholicism is so profound that it seems almost impossible to recognize them as two forms of one Christianity." From the other side of the ecclesiastical fence, it struck no one as particularly unusual when in 1954 the second General Assembly of the World Council of Churches met in Evanston, Illinois, and Chicago's Cardinal Samuel Strich issued a pastoral letter forbidding priests to attend even as reporters while urging all Catholics to stay far away.

By the late 1950s, Catholic-Protestant relations were beginning to thaw, but even then moderate voices still talked in terms of a chasm. In 1956 the Catholic Louis Bouyer's *The Spirit and Forms of Protestantism* expressed eagerness to replace prejudice with sympathy. His book conceded a great deal to various Protestant insights, but soon the language of antithesis took over. Bouyer concluded that, while the religion of Luther, Calvin, and their theological descendants contained insights which the Catholic Church needed, it was "compromised . . . irremediably" by its fatal attachment to the philosophical and theological nominalism of the sixteenth century. A similar analysis came from the Lutheran Jaroslav Pelikan in 1959. His *The Riddle of Roman Catholicism* represented a charitable effort to dispel prejudice. Yet when Pelikan came to describe the current situation, he turned instinctively to metaphors of conflict—"unconditional surrender," "the great divide," "theological alienation." Neither did he hold out high hopes for an improvement in "what we have now . . . , on both sides, a picture of the other side that is part photograph, part old daguerreotype, and part caricature."

In order to recall what was then commonplace, Americans of a certain age remember the burst of Protestant panic that appeared in 1960 when a Catholic, John F. Kennedy, became president. In that same period, well-documented reports of Catholic outrages against Protestants in Columbia, Spain, Poland, and elsewhere kept ecclesiastical tension at the boiling point.

If we fast-forward to the present—now a half-century removed

from the Second Vatican Council, which did so much to change the state of play—it is difficult to credit the depth of such negative counter-assessments. The contrast to the spirit in which Lewis and Father Calabria wrote to each other could not be more striking. Yet their spirit, as it turns out, predicted more accurately what has come to pass than did the reassertions of permanent Catholic-Protestant antagonism that filled public space even as they conducted their private correspondence.

My own experience provides only a single limited perspective that can by no means speak for a complex world situation, though it does have the advantage of first-hand immediacy. I am by no means the first active Protestant of evangelical, Reformed, or pietistic convictions to be hired by the University of Notre Dame, one of the nation's leading Catholic universities. Almost unbelievably from the perspective of 1960, quite a few like myself have not only been hired, but positively welcomed as individuals who because of our manifest faith commitments have been recruited to bolster the university's *Catholic* mission.

Of course the contemporary reality, so different from the late 1940s, does present curiosities of its own. During my nearly ten years at Notre Dame, for instance, I have had to chuckle at the current state of intra-, but also inter-, ecclesiastical relationships. Occasionally I have taken part in conversations where the strongest appreciation of something written or done by Pope John Paul II and Pope Benedict XVI came from me, the lone Protestant present. I have not yet experienced the same in conversations about Pope Francis I, but that is only because everyone at a campus like Notre Dame speaks favorably about the current pope, if perhaps for different reasons.

The point to be made for a preface to the Latin letters of C. S. Lewis is that the book now in your hands presents an early anticipation of what has become the new normal. Of course much remains that divides Catholics from Protestants, as well as Catholics from other Catholics and Protestants from other Protestants. But

positive, fruitful, self-critical, and mutually beneficial exchanges among Christian believers representing once completely alienated traditions has become the rule. One of the most historically intriguing exceptions to what had long been an exactly opposition state of affairs unfolded in the correspondence that makes up this collection. For that reason, as well as for the light it sheds on the ones who wrote the letters, it remains a timely as well as an edifying book.

Mark A. Noll, Francis A. McAnaney Professor of History at the University of Notre Dame, is the author of *Protestantism: A Very Short Introduction*, Oxford, 2007) and other books.

PREFACE

I FIRST READ THE LATIN CORRESPONDENCE BETWEEN DON GIOVANNI Calabria of Verona (1873–1954) and C. S. Lewis (1898-1963) in 1985. I was captivated and at once wrote the Summary which appeared in Volume 6 of *Seven: An Anglo-American Literary Journal*. This has been published in the USA by Crossway Books under the title *The Latin Letters of C. S. Lewis* with an Afterword by Dr. Lyle W. Dorsett of Wheaton.

I have, since the publication of *The Latin Letters*, visited Verona and there through the kindness of the Archivist Fra Elviro Dall'Ora (PSDP) have received from the Verona archives a few additional items. These I have now incorporated. Thus the present volume presents, so far as currently known, the complete text of the Correspondence. By courtesy of *Seven*, of Crossway and, at Wheaton, of Dr. Dorsett, the earlier Summary, abbreviated and slightly modified, is here reprinted, as Introduction.

The letters are given in facing Latin and English, with Notes on the Letters. A Table lists the dates.

"Te beatum dico et dicam": thus, at one point does Don Giovanni Calabria address Lewis, out of gratitude for Lewis's work as scholar, tutor and author: "I call you blessed and always shall."

Friend of the poor and tireless for unity, now it is Father John himself who, in 1988, by his beatification (Verona, 17th April) has been for ever numbered with the blessed.

ACKNOWLEDGMENTS

I acknowledge with gratitude the help which I have received from others at many points and chiefly from Dr. Barbara Reynolds, who first told me of the existence of the letters and obtained me photostats and permission to translate them.

Therewith I acknowledge the kindness of the Marion E. Wade Collection at Wheaton and of Wheaton College itself. The Archivist at Verona and members of Don Calabria's Congregation have been no less kind, especially in allowing me to use letters in their possession, provided this be done in the spirit of Don Calabria himself.

I am very much indebted to Professor Wiseman of Exeter University who at the invitation of the Trustees went over the manuscript and my translation in first draft, and contributed substantial corrections and suggestions.

Others whom I have gratefully consulted include Mr. J.E.T. Brown, Father Walter Hooper, Miss Nan Dunbar, Mrs. Teresa Moulton and, not least, Sir David Hunt.

Above all, Mr. Colin Hardie has been of constant and invaluable help throughout.

For errors and faults of style which remain, the responsibility is mine. And there are several obscurities in the manuscript and in the chronology which time may yet clear up.

Finally, I express my thanks to Miss Sadler for her indefatigable work in typing and collating both text and translation.

INTRODUCTION

When I learned – almost by chance – that there existed in America (Wheaton College) a collection of letters in Latin from C. S. Lewis to a correspondent in Italy, I was thrilled. That in our day and age Lewis should have brought off such a feat was one more feather in his cap. Doubtless there are those who even today can speak in Latin and more still who can *correspond* in it. But Lewis not only *could* correspond – he, it appeared, had actually done so, and done so in days when the art as a scholarly practice had died out.

And my second thrill was when I was able to see the letters in photostat.

They were limpid, fluent and deeply refreshing. There was a charm about them, too, and not least in the way they were "topped and tailed" – that is, in their ever-slightly-varied formalities of address and of farewell.

I noticed early on a passage in which Lewis has a characteristic tilt at the Renaissance and especially its destruction of everyday Latin in favour of a forced Classicism. In the battle between "Trojans" and "Greeks", Lewis was always with the Trojans, with the so-called dunces against the so-called humanists, with the true romantics, that is, against the false classicists. "If only", Lewis writes,

> If only that plaguey Renaissance which the Humanists brought about had not *destroyed* Latin – and destroyed it just when they were pluming themselves they were advancing it!

We should then still be able to correspond with the whole of
Europe. LETTER 3

Yet correspond Lewis could and did. One or two letters a year,
during the years 1947–1961, the majority being from Magdalen,
Oxford, and the last five from – or as from – Magdalene,
Cambridge (both incidentally, as he points out, pronounced
Maudlin) (Letter 27).

There were no photostats of the replies; and the reason for
this – it emerged from one of the last letters – gave me pause.

Evidently Lewis had been asked by the Casa Buoni Fanciulli
(The Good Children's Home) of Verona if he could let them have
the originals or else copies of the letters which he had received
from his correspondent, their Founder, the Venerable (now the
Blessed) Don Giovanni Calabria. To this Lewis replies that he cannot. Much as he would like to help, it was his custom to consign
letters to the fire two days after receipt; he had done so with Don
Calabria's letters, not because he did not value them but because
he did not wish to relinquish to posterity things worthy of a
sacred silence.

> For nowadays investigative researchers dig out all our affairs
> and sully them with the poison of "publicity" – as a bar-
> barous thing I am giving it a barbarous name. LETTER 33

This is the last thing, Lewis writes, which he would wish to
happen to Father John who, "in his humility and with a certain
holy imprudence", had confided to Lewis things which Lewis
would wish to remain undisclosed. Lewis asks that this be politely conveyed to Father Mondrone.

It is perhaps in line with this that, in one of his letters, Lewis
writes to Father John ("What a layman ought scarcely to say to a
priest"):

> You write much about your sins. Beware (permit me, my
> dearest Father, to say beware) lest humility should pass over
> into anxiety or sadness. LETTER 16

⌖ *14* ⌖

Naturally, having read Lewis's *caveat* about those who dig up private matters, I immediately put myself in the dock. Was I thinking of doing just what Lewis deplored? But the Lewis letters are already open to view. Moreover, intimate though they were in tone, they themselves did not contain any confidences which charity would wish to keep covered. On the contrary, they were to me, and might be to others, a source of renewed inspiration.

The Lewis letters are preserved in original in the Verona archives, and on a visit to the archivist, Fra Elviro Dall'Ora, in 1987 I was able to see them. As noted by Clara Sarocco in the 1987 February *Bulletin of the New York C. S. Lewis· Society,* Verona holds a few more than are on record in Wheaton, besides a few copies of typed letters from Don Calabria to Lewis.

From the letters in the Verona archives it appeared that Father John was an Italian priest in Verona, the Founder of the Casa Buoni Fanciulli, and the author of several publications, especially on the cause he was devoted to, Christian unity. He celebrated the Jubilee of his priesthood in 1951. There is also external evidence as follows.

First, there was an article in *La Civiltà Cattolica* by Father Domenico Mondrone, S.J.: "Una Gemma del Clero Italiano, Don Giovanni Calabria" (A Jewel of the Italian Clergy, Don Giovanni Calabria) which article, abridged and translated by I. G. Capaldi, was published in London under the title "God's Care-Taker" in the October 1956 issue of *The Month.* Later, Father Mondrone wrote an article, again in *La Civilta Cattolica,* "Don Giovanni e i fratelli separati"; and this subject received expanded treatment in a Lateran thesis by Eugenio dal Corso, *Il Servo di Dio, Don Giovanni Calabria e i Fratelli Separati* (The Servant of God, Don Giovanni Calabria, and the Separated Brethren). A fuller work, prefaced by Don Luigi Pedrollo and entitled *Don Giovanni Calabria, Servo di Dio,* appeared in 1958.

All of these writings vividly bring out the devoted and truly saintly life of Father John as "a champion of the charity of the

Gospel , and in particular how he founded, first, his San Zeno orphanage, the Casa Buoni Fanciulli, in 1907-08 and, later, his Congregation, The Poor Servants of Divine Providence, approved by his Bishop in 1932 and by the Pope in 1947. He died aged 81 in 1954; and this year, 1988, in Verona on 17th April, Pope John Paul pronounced his beatification.

The articles on Father John and the Separated Brethren tell of his theological and ecumenical activities, and how he reached out to unknown correspondents in his concern for Christian unity and his desire to join with others in recalling men to Christ. We learn of several other correspondents besides Lewis. But no other correspondence seems to have been so long-lasting, so affectionate, or so rewarding.

What alerted Don Calabria was the translation of *The Screwtape Letters* into Italian in 1947 (published by Arnoldo Mondadori). The work's title in Italian was *Le Lettere di Berlicche*. It so attracted Father John that he wrote to C. S. Lewis on 1st September 1947 – and their long correspondence ensued.

Born in Verona in 1873 and growing up there as a poor boy, Father Giovanni had early contacts with its Jewish community and also with Protestant acquaintances. His father died in 1886. His mother was very devout, and her support and her influence lasting. With the years, Father John's ecumenical interests grew, ending only with his death (he died after much suffering) on 4th December 1954.

Evidently Lewis was apprised of his death by the Congregation and was also sent a photograph. Acknowledging this, Lewis wrote that Father Giovanni had left the tribulations of this world and flown to our native Country, adding:

> Thank you for the photograph. His appearance is as I imagined:a conscious gravity harmoniously in accord with a certain youthful vivacity. I shall always make remembrance of him in my prayers and of your Congregation, too; and I hope you will do the same for me.   LETTER 28

Thereafter Lewis's letters continued, till within a few years of Lewis's own death, between him and Don Luigi Pedrollo (1888-1986), the inheritor of Don Calabria's place as a correspondent. The tone of Lewis's letters is uninterrupted; and they retain their interest to the last.

The letter from Don Calabria to Lewis, dated 1st September 1947 is the one which opened the correspondence. Lewis seems to have answered at once on 6th September and, hearing in return, to have written again on 20th September. The second letter extant from Verona is dated 18th September 1949; the third, 17th December 1949; the fourth is undated, and the fifth is dated 3rd September 1953. Their Latin is often rough and ready but it always carries forward with great vigour and Lewis must have relished reading it as much as he relished the use of words himself. For his part, Lewis again and again finds the right word and he is not stymied by odd ones either: "typewriter" becomes *dactylographica machina.*

Father John continually expresses joy at Lewis's messages and at his work. He freely exchanges opinions with him and he is all the time encouraging him to write more. "Certainly", he writes on 18th September 1949,

> . . . you seem to me to be called to a special mission for the good of your neighbour . . . the gifts of heart and mind which give you influence, the place which you hold among young students are sufficiently dear signs of God's will in respect of yourself. God expects from you that by word and deed you will firmly and gently bring brethren to the Gospel of Christ.
>
> LETTER 12

In response, Lewis shared with his friend his hopes and fears, his experiences and his reflections and, when requested, his views on life and world affairs. In one letter, he castigates the West for having done little, alongside missionary effort, to help China economically. But it is the theme of Christian unity which, though it does not monopolize the correspondence, sets the keynote. *Ut omnes unum sint,* that they all may be one (John XVII

21): Lewis thanks Father John for his words and his publications on this theme; for his part, he answers Father John that no day passes when he does not himself pray that prayer – and pray it from the heart.

There is no schism, Lewis agrees, without sin. It does not follow, he thinks, that sin is schism's whole cause. Tetzel, on the one side, and Henry VIII, on the other, were indeed lost men. But what of Thomas More and Tyndale? I have recently, says Lewis, read through the whole works *(sic)* of the one and the other. Both were the saintliest men whose shoes Lewis felt unworthy to unloose. But they differed; and their dissension arose not from faults of theirs or ignorance but rather from their very virtues and from their faith's truest depth. It was what was best in each that placed them most at variance. Lewis concludes that for him this is a mystery – perhaps more so, he adds, than it is for Father John. He alludes to the Psalmist: "Thy judgements are an abyss."

To write of the Pope, as Father John had, as "the point of meeting" seemed to him to beg the question since it was around the Papacy, Lewis wrote, that almost all dissension had revolved. What Lewis himself held regarding the Papacy, he does not here say. As likely as not he joined with those Anglican divines for whom the Papacy has a primacy of honour (though not jurisdiction). Elsewhere he observed that nothing would be a more powerful persuasive (he was writing before Pope John Paul II) than a Pope himself who was seen to be acting as the head of Christendom. However, pending the union of faith and of order, all the more should the union of charity be ours. And, in this spirit of charity, joint resistance against common foes is, Lewis wholeheartedly agrees, the way ahead. For:

> disputations do more to aggravate schisms than to heal them: common action, united prayer, united courage and even (if God so will) united deaths – these will make us one.
>
> LETTER 5

Having shared their minds on this subject of Christian unity,

the two correspondents, it seems, passed on to other things. But there are echoes of the subject throughout. Thus, writing of the Hitlers of our times, Lewis suggests that these may prove, by God's overruling, to have been hammers, hammers for good, used by God to weld us (us, who have refused less severe remedies) into unity. For, he writes

> . . . those who suffer the same things from the same people for the same Person can hardly fail to love each other.
>
> LETTER 3

There is one other passage in which Lewis turns to the theme of unity – and to the terrible facts of disunity – and that is when he reports that he is holiday-bound and soon to cross over to Ireland:

> . . . to my birthplace and dearest refuge, so far as loveliness of landscape goes and mildness of climate – although most dreadful because of the strife, hatred and often civil war between dissenting beliefs. There indeed both your people and ours "know not by what Spirit they are led". They take lack of charity for zeal and mutual ignorance for orthodoxy.
>
> LETTER 24

Elsewhere he writes, let us keep the bond of charity "which, alas, your people in Spain and ours in Northern Ireland do not".

From one of Father John's letters (3rd September 1953) it is evident how vibrant a chord Lewis awoke when he wrote of zeal mistaken for charity and mutual ignorance mistaken for orthodoxy. "These words has the Spirit inspired you with! I call you blessed and always shall because God wills to use you in the execution of His works" (Letter 21).

These bonds of love, needless to add, extend far beyond the realm of public affairs; and nothing is more delightful in this correspondence than the evidently growing and heart-felt affection between the two never-to-meet writers. In a letter of 17th March 1953, Lewis writes that it

. . . is a wonderful thing and a strengthening of faith that two souls differing from each other in place, nationality, language, obedience and age should have been led into a delightful friendship: so far does the order of spiritual beings transcend the material order.   LETTER 23

Throughout the letters there is a happy intermingling of serious reflection and day-to-day needs. Lewis cannot reply at once, he writes, because he is engulfed in the return of undergraduates at the beginning of term and so is experiencing the curse of our First Parent – "in the sweat of thy face shalt thou eat bread".

The seasons do not pass unnoticed, nor does the weather. In the Spring of 1948, all Nature, he writes, is visibly emblematic of the joy of Easter. Evil days notwithstanding,

Nature herself – the very face of the earth, being now renewed after its own manner at the start of Spring – bids us *Rejoice!*   LETTER 7

At times Lewis has less cheerful notes to strike:

I work under great difficulties. My house is unquiet, rent with women's quarrels. I have to dwell "in the tents of Kendar". My aged mother *(grandaeva mater),* worn out by long infirmity, is my daily care.   LETTER 9

However, if he tells Father John all this, it is not, he quickly adds, "by way of complaint but lest Father John should believe that he has the time to be writing books". Moreover, at fifty Lewis feels that his talent is decreasing and his readers less pleased than they used to be. So,

. . . if it shall please God that I write more books, blessed be He. If it shall please Him not, again, blessed be He.
          LETTER 9

Nothing in these letters is more constant than Lewis's own courageous constancy. The great truths of the Christian faith its

great topics – are frequently adduced to fortify daily life. Language which could sound trite wins our admiration under the weight of trouble. *Nil desperandum* – we smile at first, at that schoolboy phrase. But – never despair – we stay to pray, when it holds its own through suffering.

Sometimes Lewis has been accused of pastiche. I would rather call it repossession. In a current context, an old mode, a remembered phrase, can be re-appropriated and can be lived out, to fresh advantage. Lewis knew old usage; repossessed, it becomes a force in his life and in the life of others.

It is just so, too, with our age-old liturgy and the Church's calendar. In these letters, Lewis is seen to be living the liturgy and living the calendar. He tells Father John he will be remembering him at Holy Communion – and prays Father John ever to make remembrance of *him*. He writes of our going to Bethlehem at the Feast of the Nativity, and of Christ's ascension, on Ascension Day. Lewis is sometimes referred to as an Ulster Protestant. But although, writing to Father John, he writes of "yours" and "ours", because Christendom is sometimes seen as either Catholic or Reformed, the Church which he was writing from was always seeking to be *both* Catholic *and* Reformed. Lewis himself, throughout these letters, draws inspiration from Christendom's primary sources, from Holy Writ and from the early Fathers, and he always does so as from a common heritage.

Lewis would recommend his pupils to read the Vulgate as a simple way of increasing knowledge of Latin and Scripture simultaneously. In this correspondence Lewis himself quotes texts from memory, in his own Latin. He once writes that his Vulgate is not to hand. The freedom he thus uses results from mastery of his source, not unfamiliarity. When he writes about the tents of Kedar he is latinizing Coverdale (The Book of Common Prayer); when about God's judgements as an abyss, he is alluding to the Vulgate and the Septuagint. In the result, many a familiar meaning is in words of his own.

In one letter Lewis writes to Father John that of all the Deadly Sins the one which most beset him was Sloth. If this was so, the sin was overcome, powerfully, by grace, and as much by the grace of cheerfulness as of energy. Spiritually, sloth is the torpor which spreads from depression. Lewis knew depression since the time of his mother's death when he was so young. He was inspired to cast it off and to help others in doing so.

Helping others is never far from Lewis's reflections. The books which he writes he hopes will fill some gap. Father John may not find the Narnia stories of interest – but may they not please the children in his Home? Or his book on prayer: it is not for the advanced but to help the beginner. It was because he found few books on the subject for *beginners* that he "tackled the job" *(Laborem aggressus sum).* This was characteristic (Letter 19).

He is charitable to the younger generation. They may seem headstrong but they show courage. Also, are they not more compassionate than heretofore, in their caring for the poor and the afflicted? We older men, he says to Father John, must be careful not to be praisers of the past (Letter 26).

He grounds his own goodwill, and that of all men, upon its foundation in Christ. More than once he steadies himself, and Father John, by recalling Christ's words that there will be wars and rumours of wars: "see that ye be not troubled."

> Let us beware lest, while we rack ourselves in vain about the fate of Europe, we neglect either Verona or Oxford.
>
> In the poor man who knocks at my door, in my ailing mother, in the young man who seeks my advice, the Lord Himself is present. Therefore let us wash His feet.
>
> LETTER 7

Lewis does not share Father John's feeling that the times are at their worst. But, if they were, what were that but our redemption drawing nearer? However, they indeed are evil and in nothing so much as being worse than pagan times. For the pagan-before-Christ had a virtue which the apostate-from-Christ can

never have. The early pagan and the late apostate are as virginity to adultery. Many apostates have fallen away not only from the law of Christ but from the law of Nature too. For, whereas Faith gained perfects Nature, Faith lost corrupts it.

Clearly one of Lewis's best-loved books was Thomas à Kempis's *The Imitation of Christ,* and some of its spirit has passed into these letters. But Lewis cannot trace in *The Imitation* a quotation he expected to find there – and does Father John know the source?

> *Amor est ignis jugiter ardens,* Love is a fire continuously burn
> ing. LETTER 17

To Father John, Lewis reports two great experiences. One was his own, one a friend's. His own he suggests he may owe to prayers by Father John on his behalf. The experience, in 1951, was a sudden and profound awareness of forgiveness of sins, of his own sins, and his own deliverance:

> I long *believed that I believed* in the forgiveness of sins. But suddenly (on St Mark's Day) this truth appeared in my mind with such manifest light that I perceived that never before (and that after many confessions and absolutions) had I believed it with my whole heart. LETTER 16

Lewis then goes on to request the liberty of counselling Father John. Do not let humility and contrition pass over into sadness. For Christ had abolished the "handwriting" *(chirographia)* that was against us. Twice Lewis excuses himself – was he not a layman and a junior? But, out of the mouths of babes. Indeed, once, in Balaam's case, out of the mouth of an ass! Finally, at the end of his filial entreaty he again asks Father John pardon, this time for his *balbutiones,* his stammerings (Letter 16).

The second experience concerned Lewis's friend, his aged Oxford confessor. It was an experience, and an example, of holy

dying. I feel orphaned, Lewis writes, because my aged confessor and most loving father in Christ has just died.

> While he was celebrating at the altar, suddenly after a most sharp but (thanks be to God) very brief attack of pain, he expired and his last words were "I come, Lord Jesus".
>
> LETTER 17

Lewis's aged confessor, when summoned to his Exodus, most gladly responded.

As you read these letters you get an ever-growing sense of the significance which should be attached to prayer. Lewis uses the word *insta*. Persevere with? Press on with? Remember its echoes in the Epistles: "patient in tribulation, continuing instant in prayer." *In tribulations patientes: Orationi instantes* (Romans XIII 12).

Lewis puts to Father John the same difficulty which he later put to the Oxford Clerical Society in his paper on 8th December 1953, "Petitionary Prayer: a problem without an answer". How can we pray "nothing doubting" while at the same time praying (with implied doubt) "Thy will be done"? It does not appear that Lewis received any answer which, to his mind, resolved the difficulty.

The combination of old and new in a Christian synthesis was something Lewis always valued, and it was something, too, which in his own way he also exemplified. It is not therefore surprising that in these letters along with scriptural allusion we find, side by side, classical quotation. Sometimes this juxtaposition produces a novel effect. *Sursum Corda,* lift up your hearts! We are not expecting this quotation from the liturgy to be followed, but followed it is and that immediately, by Virgil:

forsan et haec olim meminisse juvabit   (*Aeneid* I 203)

How familiar yet how vivid! "Perhaps one day it will be a joy to recall even this." The great utterance takes on a fresh vigour from its new Christian context.

As the letters approach the 1960s, so there is a sense of change, not because Lewis, from 1954 onwards, is writing to a new correspondent following Father John's death, but because of actual changes in Lewis's own world. And, first of all, the move from Oxford to Cambridge.

Earlier, Lewis had said that Italy had one advantage over Britain. In Italy, Communists declared themselves to be atheists and so people knew where everyone stood. In England, however, extremists all too often claim to be advancing the kingdom of God and present themselves in sheep's clothing.

When it comes to Oxford and Cambridge, Lewis (before he had moved to Cambridge) wrote:

> The Christian Faith counts for more, I think, among Cambridge men than among us; the Communists are rarer and those plaguey philosophers whom we call Logical Positivists are not so powerful.   LETTER 27

Now a grief emerges. The word *aerumna* re-appears (16th April 1960) and does so with stark brevity: "I am in much trouble." Lewis does not specify. But earlier he had said how, after a remission of two years, his wife Joy's lethal disease has returned. Even so, he adds, you would not believe how many joys have been experienced amid these troubles. "And what wonder? For has He not promised to comfort those who mourn?" (Letter 31). So here. "I am in much trouble. None the less let us lift up our hearts: for Christ is risen" (Letter 32). It is impossible, reading these letters, not to be moved equally by grief and admiration. Going through the vale of misery what fortitude Lewis shows. Nor does he hesitate to use a traditional phrase or to utter a customary observation. This was characteristic and intentional. We are to follow the Way. Even in the Valley of the Shadow, Lewis does not give up. He bears it out, even "to the edge of doom". And why? Because, to quote Shakespeare, "Love's not Time's fool".

It seems to me that there is a special poignancy in his Latin at the close, a Latin the very rhythm of which is infinitely moving. But there is no want of poignancy in the English either. Surely our hearts and prayers will follow Lewis as he writes this last sentence of these letters of his, some eight months after Joy's death, on 8th April in the Year of Our Salvation 1961:

> I know that you will pour out your prayers both for my most dearly-longed-for wife and also for me who – now bereaved and as it were halved – journey on, through this Vale of Tears, alone. LETTER 34

Looking back over this C. S. Lewis/Don Calabria correspondence you see that Lewis and Father John unite with each other in teaching a ministry of charity. Correspondence was itself a part of this ministry of theirs. It must often have been exacting yet it was also sustaining. Its essence was mutual intercession.

Christianly speaking, no farewells, Lewis used to say, are final. So, in conclusion, let us, together as it were with Father John and with Lewis himself, share in that affirmation of hope which Lewis, writing from Magdalen College, Oxford, on 14th January 1949, addresses to his "Father most-beloved", in Verona:

> Now indeed mountains and seas divide us; nor do I know what your appearance is in the body. On some day hereafter, in the resurrection of the body, and in that renewal beyond our telling, God grant that we may meet. LETTER 9

Martin Moynihan

THE LATIN LETTERS
BETWEEN
C. S. LEWIS
and
DON GIOVANNI CALABRIA
(1947–1954)

1

Praeclarissime ut Frater,

Gratia et pax Domini nostri Jesu Christi sit semper nobiscum. – Qui nunc Tibi scripturus humilis est sacerdos veronensis (Italia), cui Divina Providentia abhinc XL annos opus commisit pro pueris et adolescentibus, vel orphanis vel utcunque omni ope et quolibet auxilio destitutis, gratis colligendis, ut artes addiscant quibus maturiori aetate sibi sufficere valeant; ad eos autem nutriendos et alendos subsidia, secura ac filiali fiducia, ab ipsa Divina Providentia expectamus, juxta illud sancti Evangelii: "Quaerite primum regnum Dei et justitiam eius, et haec omnia adjicientur vobis."

Inspiratio Tibi scribendi mihi venit dum legerem optimum tuum librum, cui italice titulus: "Le lettere di Berlicche"; ratio autem est ut meam Tibi mentem aperiam circa maximi problema momenti, ad quod solvendum, vel saltem ad ejus solutionem favendam, maturiora esse tempora quam antea mihi videntur; hodie enim, propter hanc bellici furoris prope universalem conflagrationem, multa intersaepta subversa sunt, tot aerumnis ac doloribus mundus tamquam aratus ager factus est, multae generales opiniones immutatae, rivalitates imminutae, ac praesertim aspiratio ex omni parte apparet magna omnium populorum reformandi; haec omnia praemissa constituere videntur ad alterum quod supra jam dixi problema solvendum, scilicet dissidentium fratrum quam maxime exoptatus reditus ad unitatem Corporis Christi, quod est Ecclesia.

1

Most distinguished brother (as it were),

The grace and peace of our Lord Jesus Christ be with us always.

He who is now about to write to you is a humble priest of Verona (Italy) to whom Divine Providence forty years ago committed the task of gathering together boys and youths, either orphans or destitute of any means of support, so that they may be given skills which will enable them to maintain themselves when grown up.

For the contributions needed for feeding and caring for them, we look with sure and filial confidence to Divine Providence itself, according to that word of the Holy Gospel: "Seek ye first the Kingdom of God and His righteousness and all these things will be added unto you."

The inspiration of writing to you came to me while I was reading your excellent book called in Italian *Le Lettere di Berlicche*. My purpose is to open my mind to you regarding a problem of the greatest importance, to solve which (or at least help towards a solution) the times seem to me riper than before. For today, because of this almost universal conflagration of war-madness many boundaries are overthrown, the world is like a field ploughed up with so many troubles and sufferings, many general opinions are changed and rivalries diminished and, in particular, on every side, there appears a great aspiration of all peoples towards reform.

Anhelitus hic est Sacratissimi Cordis Jesu, in illa ad Patrem antequam pateretur oratione manifestatus: "Ut omnes unum sint."

Omnibus quidem interest hunc divinum anhelitum complere; ego candide Tibi fateor, a primis annis mei sacerdotii ad hoc magnum problema totis viribus animum vertisse; atque ita "Octavam precum pro unitate Ecclesiae" diebus 18–25 Januarii habendam propagare coepi; in una domorum nostrae Congregationis diurnam Eucharisticam adorationem ac preces publice faciendas pro unitate ab Episcopo Diocesano impetravi; ad eundem finem literas hue illuc pro opportunitate mittere humiliter curavi, et alia similia opera, in mea paupertate, peragere studui.

Sed Tu quoque mihi videris in Domino multum conferre posse, magna qua polles auctoritate, non solum in nobilisima Patria Tua, sed etiam in aliis terris. Quomodo autem et quibus mediis Tuae relinquo prudentiae; pauper ut sum ego enixe orare promitto, ut Deus et Dominus noster Jesus Christus illuminare et confortare dignetur, ut aliquid majoris momenti perficere queas in vinea Domini, ut tandem videre possit: "Unum ovile et unus Pastor."

Veniam obsecro mihi concedas, pro libertate qua Tecum uti ausus sum; Si quid vero mihi scribere volueris, scito pergratam rem mihi Te facturum.

Tuis orationibus enixe me commendo, necnon pueros et fratres mihi commissos; hanc caritatem Tibi rependere, pro paucitate virium mearum, quotidie praesertim in augustissimo Missae sacrificio celebrando dulce mihi erit.

In fraterno amplexu, benedictionem Dei Patris, et Filii, et Spiritus Sancti, per intercessionem Beatae Mariae Virginis, Tibi ac Tuis adprecans, me humiliter signo Tuus in Corde Jesu. . . .

DON CALABRIA

All these things seem to constitute anticipations of the solution of that other problem which I have already referred to: namely that of the dissenting brethren whose return to the unity of the Body of Christ, which is the Church, is most greatly desired.

This is the sigh of the Most Sacred Heart of Jesus manifested in that prayer of His to the Father before He suffered: "that they all may be one."

It concerns all of us that this divine sigh should be fulfilled. I candidly confess to you that from the first years of my priesthood I have turned my mind with all my strength to this great problem. And so I have begun to propagate the holding of an "octave of prayers for the unity of the Church" from the 18th to the 25th of January. In one of the houses of our Congregation I have succeeded in obtaining from the diocesan Bishop permission for daylong adoration of the Sacrament, and the offering of public prayers for the sake of unity. To the same end, I have humbly taken the trouble, as opportunity offers, to send letters here and there, and have tried to perform other similar tasks in my poor way.

But you also seem to me to be able to contribute much in the Lord, with your great influence not only in your own most noble country but even in other lands. How and by what means I leave to your prudence. Poor as I am, I promise to pray strenuously that God and our Lord Jesus Christ will see fit to illuminate and strengthen you that you may be able to perform something of greater moment in the Lord's vineyard, so that at last it may be seen that "there is one fold and one Shepherd".

I pray that you will pardon me for the liberty I have ventured to take with you. If indeed there is anything you would like to write to me, be assured that you would be doing something I should greatly welcome.

I commend myself earnestly to your prayers and commend also the boys and brothers committed to my charge. To repay you this act of charity to the measure of my powers, poor though they

2

Magdalen College
Oxford

6th September 1947

Reverende Pater,

Epistolam tuam plenam caritate et benevolentia grato animo accepi. Scito et mihi causam doloris et materiam orationum esse hoc schisma in corpore Domini, gravissimum intrantibus scandalum, quod etiam omnes fideles reddit debiliores ad communem hostem repellendum. Ego tamen laicus, immo laicissimus, minimeque peritus in profundioribus sacrae theologiae quaestionibus. Conatus sum id facere quod solum facere posse mihi videor: id est, quaestiones subtiliores de quibus Romana Ecclesia et Protestantes inter se dissentiunt omnino relinquere (episcopis et eruditis viris tractandas) propriis vero libris ea exponere quae adhuc, Dei gratia, post tanta peccata tantosque errores communia sunt. Neque inutile opus: vulgus enim video ignorare de quam multis etiam nunc consentimus – adeo ut hominem inveni qui credebat vos negare Trinitatem Dei! Praeter

be, especially in daily celebrating the most august sacrifice of the Mass, will be a joy to me.

In brotherly embrace and entreating, for you and yours, the blessing of God the Father, the Son and the Holy Ghost, by the intercession of the Blessed Virgin Mary, I humbly sign myself, yours in the Heart of Jesus. . . .

DON CALABRIA

2

Magdalen College
Oxford

6th September 1947

Reverend Father,

Thank you for your letter, full of love and goodwill. Be assured that for me too schism in the Body of Christ is both a source of grief and a matter for prayers, being a most serious stumbling block to those coming in and one which makes even the faithful weaker in repelling the common foe. However, I am a layman, indeed the most lay of laymen, and least skilled in the deeper questions of sacred theology. I have tried to do the only thing that I think myself able to do: that is, to leave completely aside the subtler questions about which the Roman Church and Protestants disagree among themselves – things which are to be treated of by bishops and learned men – and in my own books to expound, rather, those things which still, by God's grace, after so many sins and errors, are shared by us. Nor is this a pointless task; for I find that people are unaware how many matters we

illud opus, semper putavi mihi quam maxime cum omnibus qui se Christianos appellant fraternaliter conversandum: id quod si omnes strenue fecerint, nonne licet sperare eam dilectionis et operationum unitatem multis annis praecedere, necnon fovere, seriorem doctrinarum redintegrationem? Tertio loco restant (quod validissimum est) orationes.

Consuetudo latine scribendi mihi per multos annos non usitata! Si quem soloecismum fecerim veniam peto.

Oremus pro invicem. Cordialiter paternae tuae caritati me commendo in Domino nostro.

C. S. LEWIS

3

Magdalen College
Oxford

20th September 1947

Reverende Pater –

Alteram tuam epistolam, 15 die Sept. scriptam, grato animo accepi.

Hora, ut dicis, vere Satanae est: sed spei nonnullas scintillas in tenebris video.

Communia pericula, communes aerumnae, commune fere omnium hominum in gregem Christi odium et contemptus pos

even now agree on – so much so that I have come across someone who believed that you deny the Three in One God! Over and above that work, it has always seemed to me that I should maintain as much fraternal intercourse as possible with all those who call themselves Christians. If all were actively to do this, might we not hope that this unity of love and action over many years would precede – not to say foster – an eventual re-unification of doctrines. Thirdly, there remain – what is most efficacious – prayers.

The practice of writing in Latin is one which for many years I have not kept up! If I have committed any solecism, I ask pardon.

Let us pray for each other. With all my heart I commend myself to your fatherly love in Our Lord.

C. S. LEWIS

3

Magdalen College
Oxford

20th September 1947

Reverend Father,

I was glad to receive your further letter written on the 15th Sept.

The hour, as you say, is indeed Satan's hour. But I see some sparks of hope in the darkness.

Common perils, common burdens, an almost universal hatred and contempt for the Flock of Christ can, by God's Grace,

sunt, Dei gratia, multum conferre ad sanandas divisiones nostras; qui enim eadem, ab eisdem, pro eodem, patiuntur, vix possunt non amare inter se. Equidem crederem Domini in animo esse (postquam leniora medicamina recusavimus) nos ipsa persecutione et angustiis in unitatem cogere. Satanas ille procul dubio nihil aliud est quam malleus in manu benevoli et severi Dei.

Omnes enim aut volentes aut nolentes voluntatem Dei faciunt: Judas et Satanas ut organa aut instrumenta, Johannes et Petrus ut filii.

Etiam nunc videmus aut majorem caritatem aut certe minus odium inter divisos Christianos esse quam fuit ante C annos: cujus rei mihi videtur (sub Deo) principalis causa esse gliscens superbia et immanitas infidelium. Hitlerus, insciens et nolens, maxime ecclesiae profuit!

Libros quos tu te missurum esse pollicitus es cum gratiarum actione expecto. Ceterorum meorum operum nullum in Italica lingua exstat: alioquin missurus eram.

Utinam pestifera ilia "Renascentia" quam Humanistae effecerunt non destruxerit (dum erigere eam se jactabant) Latinam: adhuc possemus toti Europae scribere.

Orationes tuas, dilecte pater, adhuc oro. Vale,

C. S. LEWIS

contribute much to the healing of our divisions. For those who suffer the same things from the same people for the same Person can scarcely not love each other.

Indeed I could well believe that it is God's intention, since we have refused milder remedies, to compel us into unity, by persecution even and hardship. Satan is without doubt nothing else than a hammer in the hand of a benevolent and severe God. For all, either willingly or unwillingly, do the will of God: Judas and Satan as tools or instruments, John and Peter as sons.

Even now we see more charity, or certainly less hatred, between separated Christians than there was a century ago. The chief cause of this (under God) seems to me to be the swelling pride and barbarity of the unbelievers. Hitler, unknowingly and unwillingly, greatly benefited the Church!

The books which you have promised to send me I await with gratitude. None of my other writings has been translated into Italian. Otherwise I would have sent them.

If only that plaguey "Renaissance" which the Humanists brought about had not *destroyed* Latin (and destroyed it just when they were pluming themselves that they were reviving it), we should then still be able to correspond with the whole of Europe.

I still ask, dear Father, for your prayers.

Farewell,

C. S. LEWIS

4

Magdalen College
Oxford

3rd October 1947

Reverende Pater –

Duos libros (Amare et Apostolica Vivendi Forma) grato animo accepi. Nomen auctoris non invenio sed puto vestros esse. Lectionem incipere adhuc non potui: nunc enim hora est negotiorum plenissima, qua iuvenes ex feriis in collegium redeunt et nos magistri sentimus primi parentis maledictionem *in sudore vultus* etc.! Futura otia et voluptatem legendi vestros libros expectamus. Vale et habe me semper in orationibus tuis,

C. S. LEWIS

5

Magdalen College
Oxford

25th November 1947

Dilecte Pater – Quamquam vernacula Italica facilior et magis nota mihi est apud Boiardum et Ariostum quam apud hodiernos tractata, *Ut omnes unum sint* grato animo perlegi: in quo multa

4

Magdalen College
Oxford

3rd October 1947

Reverend Father,

I have received with pleasure two books *Amare* and *Apostolice Vivendi Forma.* I do not find the name of the author but I think they are your Congregation's.

I cannot yet begin reading them: because now the time is completely occupied by the return of undergraduates to the College after the vacation and we tutors experience the curse of our First Parent, *in the sweat of thy face etc.!*

We look forward to some leisure time to come – and to the pleasure of reading your books.

Farewell, and have me ever in your prayers.

C. S. LEWIS

5

Magdalen College
Oxford

25th November 1947

Dear Father,

Although Italian (the Italian vernacular) is easier for me – and better known – in the pages of Boiardo or Ariosto than the Italian

placent. Nonnulla autem nequeo concedere de quibus pauca rescribam, filiali licentia qua (credo) me uti volebas.

1. De omnipotentia verbi Domini qui ipse Verbum est, quatenus est verbum imperans, consentio. De omnipotentia ejusdem verbi, quatenus oratio est, haesito. Potest enim responderi quod ipse in horto Gethsemane oravit nec impetravit. Deinde, nonne est terribilis veritas, liberum arbitrium mali hominis posse Dei voluntati resistere? Omnipotentiam enim suam modo quodam restrinxit ipso facto creandi liberam creaturam et legimus nescio qua regione Dominum *non potuisse* miracula facere quia defuit fides in hominibus.

2. Totam causam schismatis in peccato esse non pro certo habeo. Concedo nullum schisma esse sine peccato, sed altera propositio alteram haud necessarie consequitur. Ex vestris Tetzel, ex nostris Henricus VIII, perditi homines erant: adde, si vis, ex vestris Papam Leonem, ex nostris Lutherum (quamquam egomet de ambobus mitiorem sententiam darem) sed quid sentiam de vestro Thoma Moro, de nostro Gulielmo Tyndale? Tota opera et hujus et illius nuper perlegi. Ambo mihi videntur esse viri sanctissimi et toto corde amare Dominum: neque hujus nec illius caligas solvere dignus sum. Attamen dissentiunt et (id quod me torquet et attonitum habet) illa dissensio mihi videtur non ex vitiis nec ex ignorantia eorum, immo ex virtutibus et fidei eorum penetralibus oriri – ita ut quo optimi sunt eo maxime dissentiunt. Credo Dei judicium de hac dissensione altius absconditum esse quam tibi videtur: etenim judicia ejus abyssus.

3. Quo scribis Papam esse *il punto d'incontro* fere committis (liceat mihi venia vestra dicere) id quod logici vocant *petitionem principii*. Nam de nihilo magis quam de auctoritate Papae dissentimus: ex qua dissensione ceterae fere omnes dependent.

Quo scribis nos omnes debere quam celerrime contra communem hostem (vel hostes "nomen Legio est") opponere unitatem caritatis et morum Christianorum, toto corde consentio. Disputationes magis aggravant schismata quam sanant: communis

of modern authors, I have read with pleasure *"Ut omnes unum sint"*: and much I agree with. Some things, however, I cannot agree with and I shall write back briefly about these, with that filial liberty which I believe you wished me to exercise.

1. About the omnipotence of the Word of God who Himself is the Word: as far as it is a word of command, I agree. As far as it is a word of prayer, I hesitate. For it can be replied that He Himself in the Garden of Gethsemane entreated but did not obtain. Next, is it not a frightening truth that the free will of a bad man can resist the will of God? For He has, after a fashion, restricted His own Omnipotence by the very fact of creating free creatures; and we read that the Lord was *not able* to do miracles in some place because people's faith was wanting.

2. That the whole cause of schism lies in sin I do not hold to be certain. I grant that no schism is without sin but the one proposition does not necessarily follow the other. From your side Tetzel, from ours Henry VIII, were lost men: and, if you like, Pope Leo from your side and from ours Luther (although for my own part I would pass on both a lighter sentence). But what would I think of your Thomas More or of our William Tyndale? All the writings of the one and all the writings of the other I have lately read right through. Both of them seem to me most saintly men and to have loved God with their whole heart: I am not worthy to undo the shoes of either of them. Nevertheless they disagree and (what racks and astounds me) their disagreement seems to me to spring not from their vices nor from their ignorance but rather from their virtues and the depths of their faith, so that the more they were at their best the more they were at variance. I believe the judgement of God on their dissension is more profoundly hidden than it appears to you to be: for His Judgements are indeed an abyss.

3. Where you write that the Pope is "the point of meeting" you almost commit (if your people will forgive my saying so) what logicians call a *petitio principii* (begging the question). For

operatio, oratio, fortitudo, communes (si Deus voluerit) mortes pro Christo adunabunt. Dixit Dominus "si quis fecerit voluntatem Patris, doctrinam sciet" (meis verbis exprimo sensum quia Novum Testamentum latine redditum hodie sub manibus non est). Faciendo veritatem quam iam scimus, in veritatem quam adhuc ignoramus progrediamur. Tunc procul dubio unum erimus: veritas enim una

Oremus pro invicem: et pro Gallia quae sub periculis jacet. Vale, in Domino

C. S. LEWIS

6

Magdalen College
Oxford

13th January 1948

Dilectissime Pater,

Grato animo accepi salutationes tuas et vota tua. "Prosint omina" scripsisti et re vera omina fuisse invenio. Nuper enim (quamquam externa meae vitae conditio in melius non mutata est) placuiit Domino tranquilitatem magnam, immo hilaritatem, in meum animum infundere. Gratias ago cum timore, quippe qui in mente infixam teneam illam salubrem sententiam in libro *De*

we disagree about nothing more than the authority of the Pope: on which disagreement almost all the others depend.

Where you write that we should all as speedily as possible oppose the common foe (or foes, their name is Legion) with the unity of Charity and Christian living, I agree with my whole heart. Disputations do more to aggravate schism than to heal it: united action, prayer, fortitude and (should God so will) united deaths for Christ – *these* will make us one. The Lord has said "If anyone will do the will of my Father, he shall know the doctrine" (I put the sense into my own words because today my Vulgate is not to hand). By doing the truth which we already know, let us make progress towards the truth which as yet we are ignorant of. Then, without doubt, we shall be one: for truth is one.

Let us pray for each other: and for France, lying in danger as she does.

Farewell in the Lord,

C. S. LEWIS

6

Magdalen College
Oxford

13th January 1948

Dearest Father,

Thank you for your salutations and your good wishes. "May the omens be favourable" you have written; and I find that in truth there have been good omens. For recently (although the outward condition of my life has not changed for the better) it has pleased God to pour into my soul great tranquility – I may even say gaiety. I give thanks not without apprehension as one who

Imitatione Christi "memento in gratia quid sine gratia sis". Utinam in aeternam constantiam sine vicissitudinis umbrâ pervenisse-mus! Octavam instare precum non ignorabam et valde probo. Pro Gallia nuper servata ex tantis tam corporalibus quam spiritual-ibus periculis gratias agamus. In quotidianis meis orationibus locum semper habes, et medicus quidam Lodetti Veronensis qui nuper fraterna epistola me confortavit. Fortasse vir tibi notus. Vale, care pater, et semper memoriam facias

tui conservi in Christo

C. S. LEWIS

7

Magdalen College
Oxford

27th March 1948

Dilectissime Pater,

Epistolam tuam plenam (ut soles) caritate grato anima accepi. Dura et inquieta sunt omnia – bella et rumores belli – fortasse non *hora novissima* sed certi *tempora pessima.* Attamen Apostolus iterum atque iterum jubet "gaudete". Ipsa naturalis mundi facies jam vere novo renovata proprio modo suo idem jubet. Credo homines hujus aetatis (et inter eos te, pater, et me) nimium cog-itare de gentium statu, de rerum saecularium summa. Nonne monet nos auctor *Imitationis* ne nimis implicemur talibus rebus? Non reges, non senatores sumus. Caveamus ne dum frustra de

keeps firmly in mind that salutary observation in *The Imitation of Christ* "remember in Grace what you would be without Grace". Would that we had attained to everlasting constancy with no shadow of turning!

I was not unaware of the approaching Octave, of Prayers for Unity, and I strongly approve of it.

For France, recently saved from such dangers, alike physical and spiritual, let us give thanks.

In my daily prayers you have ever a place and with you a certain physician, Dr. Lodetti of Verona who recently encouraged me in a brotherly letter. Perhaps he is known to you. Farewell, dear Father, and may you ever make remembrance of

Your fellow servant in Christ

C. S. LEWIS

7

Magdalen College
Oxford

27th March 1948

Dearest Father,

I was glad to receive your letter – so full (as is your wont) of Charity.

Everywhere things are troubling and uneasy – wars and rumours of war: perhaps not the final hour but certainly times most evil.

Nevertheless, the Apostle again and again bids us "Rejoice". Nature herself bids us do so, the very face of the earth being now renewed, after its own manner, at the start of Spring.

I believe that the men of this age (and among them you

Europae fato cruciamur negligamus aut Veronam aut Oxoniam. In paupere qui ad meam portam pulsat, in matre aegrotante, in juvene qui consilium meum petit, ipse Dominus adest: ergo ejus pedes lavemus. Semper credidi recte sentire illum infidelem Voltaire dum monet *Hortum tuum exerce:* necnon Gulielmum Dunbar (Scoticum poetam qui XVmo saeculo floruit) dum dicit

> Vir, place Creatori tuo, et hilari esto animo;
> Totum vero hunc mundum unius aestimemus assis.

Cras celebrabimus gioriosam Christi resurectionem: tui in sacra communione memor ero. Abeste lacrimae, timores, taedia! Natura nostra cum ipsa Deitate aeterno conjugio adunata in caelum caelorum ascendit. Adhuc nos "miseros" vocare impietatis esset. Immo, HOMO est creatura cui inviderent angeli si invidere possint. Sursum corda: *forsan et haec olim meminisse juvabit.*

Pro litania ista a Cardinale Merry composita, multas gratias ago. Num sciebas omnes temptationes contra quas preces fundit mihi nimium et diu cognitas esse? *Desiderio di essere stimato . . timore di essere rifiutato . . .* uhé, compungis me!

Semper oremus pro invicem. Vale.

C. S. LEWIS

Father, and myself) think too much about the state of nations and the situation of the world. Does not the author of *The Imitation* warn us against involving ourselves too much with such things?

We are not kings, we are not senators. Let us beware lest, while we torture ourselves in vain about the fate of Europe, we neglect either Verona or Oxford.

In the poor man who knocks at my door, in my ailing mother, in the young man who seeks my advice, the Lord Himself is present: therefore let us wash His feet.

I have always believed that Voltaire, infidel though he was, thought aright in that admonition of his to cultivate your own garden: likewise William Dunbar (the Scottish poet who flourished in the 15th century) when he said

> Man, please thy Maker and be merry;
> This whole world rate we at a penny!

Tomorrow we shall celebrate the glorious Resurrection of Christ. I shall be remembering you in the Holy Communion. Away with tears and fears and troubles! United in wedlock with the eternal Godhead Itself, our nature ascends into the Heaven of Heavens. So it would be impious to call ourselves "miserable". On the contrary, Man is a creature whom the Angels – were they capable of envy – would envy. Let us lift up our hearts! "At some future time perhaps even these things it will be a joy to recall."

For the Litany composed by Cardinal Merry many thanks. You did not know, did you, that all the temptations against which he pours forth these prayers I have long been exceedingly conscious of? *Desiderio di essere stimato . . . timore di essere rifiutato* * . . . *Touché,* you pink me!

Let us pray for each other always. Farewell.

C. S. LEWIS

* Longing to be thought well of . . . fear of being rejected

8

Collegium Stae Mariae Magdalenae
apud Oxonienses

Aug. X a.s. 1948

Grato animo, Pater dilectissime, litteras tuas accepi.

Cur dubitas te locum tuum in orationibus meis et adhuc habere et habiturum esse? Nostram rempublicam in lubrico versari recte judicas. Apud nos conflictus est haud acrior quam in Italia sed quodam modo difficilior. Vestri *Sinistrales* (ut ita dicam!) Atheismum suum confitentur, immo jactant, lupi sunt et lupi esse videntur. Nos patimur multitudinem luporum ovilibus vestimentis vestitorum. Eorum qui injustitiam faciunt in re politica multi dicunt se Regnum Domini aedificare; nec dicunt solum sed fortasse credunt. Non enim nostri est corda discernere et caritas nihil malitiae imputat quod potest ex simplici stultitia et ignorantia evenire – "fert omnia, credit omnia". Mihi quidem videtur nihil in hoc statu rerum molestius esse quam quod quotidiana pugna contra odium (non dico inimicorum sed nostrum) nos exercet. Nunc etiam novae minae rumoresque belli oriuntur. Attamen saepe recurro ad apostolicum illud verbum "nulla temptatio nobis accidit nisi quae communis est hominibus – nondum ad sanguinem etc.". Gratias debemus agere pro omni fortuna; si "bona" est quia bona est, si "mala" quia operatur in nobis patientiam, humilitatem, et contemptum saeculi et spem aeternae Patriae.

Vale: semper oremus pro invicem.

C. S. LEWIS

8

from the College of St Mary Magdalen
Oxford

10th August in the year of salvation 1948

Thank you, dearest Father, for your letter.

Why doubt that you still hold, and shall hold, a place in my prayers?

You rightly judge that our country is in a hazardous state. With us the struggle is not more intense than in Italy but in one way it is more difficult.

Your Leftists – your Sinisters, to put it like that – declare their atheism. Even boast of it. Wolves they are and wolves they are seen to be.

We endure a pack of wolves, dressed in sheep's clothing. Of those who work injustice in politics many say they are building the Kingdom of God. Nor do they merely say it, they perhaps believe it. For we do not have the ability to read hearts, and Charity does not ascribe to malice that which can result from simple foolishness and ignorance – it "beareth all things, believeth all things".

To me nothing in this state of affairs seems more grievous than the struggle against hatred in which we are daily engaged – I will not say the hatred of enemies but of our own people.

Now indeed new threats and rumours of war are arising. Nevertheless I often recur to that word of the Apostle: no temptation has befallen you except what is common to men – "not yet unto blood, etc."

We ought to give thanks for all fortune: if it is "good", because it is good, if "bad" because it works in us patience, humility and the contempt of this world and the hope of our eternal country.

Farewell: and let us pray for one another always.

C. S. LEWIS

9

Magdalen College
Oxford

Jan. XIV. 1949

Laeto animo, Pater dilectissime, epistolam tuam in die Natali
Domini scriptam accepi eo gratiorem quia tam solemni horâ me
in memoria habere voluisti. Noli dubitare quin locum usitatum in
orationibus meis teneas. Nunc vero montes et maria nos dividunt
nec scio quâ sis formâ corporis; placeat Deo ut olim in resurrec-
tione corporum et inenarrabili illâ novitate congrediamur.

Quod ad meos labores pertinet, nollem te spe inani fallere.
Iam quinquagesimum annum ago. Fervorem scribendi et
priscum quidquid erat ingenii decrescere sentio: neque (credo)
lectoribus, ut solebam, placeo. Multis aerumnis laboro. Domus
mea inquieta, muliebribus rixis vastata, *inter tabernacula Kedar
habitandum est,* Grandaeva mater, longa valetudine confecta, diur-
nae curae mihi est.

Ora pro me, Pater, ut semper in mente habeam praeclaram
istam sententiam "si vis pacificare alios, tene *te* in pace". Haec
scribo non quasi querelas sed ne forte credas me opera componere. Si Deo placuerit ut plura scribam, benedictus sit; si non
placuerit, iterum benedictus sit. Fortasse animae meae saluberri-
mum erit et famam et ingenium perdere ne in vanam gloriam
(malam pestem) lapsurus essem.

De istis parvis "magnis viris" quorum mentionem fecisti,
tacebo. Magna minantur et magna pollicentur; utraque (fortasse)
vana. Sollicitudo de rebus futuris frustra angit mentes mortales.
Attamen, confiteor, saepe cogimur dicere "Quousque, Domine?"
    Vale,

C. S. LEWIS

9

Magdalen College
Oxford

14th January 1949

With a joyful heart, dearest Father, I received your letter written on the day of the Lord's Nativity – all the more welcome for this, that you were willing to remember me in so solemn an hour.

Do not doubt that you hold your accustomed place in my prayers. Now, indeed, mountains and seas divide us; nor do I know what your appearance is in the body. On some day hereafter, in the resurrection of the body, and in that renewal beyond our telling, God grant that we may meet.

As for my own work, I would not wish to deceive you with vain hope. I am now in my fiftieth year. I feel my zeal for writing, and whatever talent I originally possessed, to be decreasing; nor (I believe) do I please my readers as I used to. I labour under many difficulties. My house is unquiet and devastated by women's quarrels. I have *to dwell in the tents of Kedar.* My aged mother, worn out by long infirmity, is my daily care. Pray for me, Father, that I ever bear in mind that profoundly true maxim: "if thou wish to bring others to peace, keep thyself in peace."

These things I write not as complaints but lest you should believe I am writing books. If it shall please God that I write more books, blessed be He. If it shall not please Him, again, blessed be He. Perhaps it will be the most wholesome thing for my soul that I lose both fame and skill lest I were to fall into that evil disease, vainglory.

About these little "big men" of whom you make mention, I shall keep silent. They threaten much, they promise much, and equally, perhaps, in vain. Concern for the future distresses mortal

10

Casa Buoni Fanciulli
Verona

PASCHA d.ni '49 17th April 1949

Dilectissime in Christo,

Gratia et pax Christi exultet in corde tuo.

Dies sollemnes propinquant, quibus Resurrectionem Domini JESU celebramus. Mens mea ad te cotidie est, praesertim his diebus auspiciorum ad fratres et amicos. Pro te a Domino precor ut vota et desideria tua omnino adimpleantur.

Domini Jesus det tibi Suam pacem in osculo dilectionis! Te adjuvet in operibus bonis multiplicandis ad profectum tuae curae commissorum, ut cos ad caelestia desideria erigas in adipiscenda humana scientia. Super te, et super familiam tuam, splendeat jugiter sol laetitiae et jucunditatis in Domino; ut dies bonos et prosperos ducatis hac vita transeunte; ac tandem suo tempore Paradisum felicitatis aeternae ingredi valeatis, meritis onusti bonorum operum!

Haec vota mea in Paschate nostro.

Tempora bona veniant! Vox quidem Dei continuo ad nos clamat; ad mundum clamat, ut remotis peccatis regnum Dei

minds in vain. However, we are often, I confess, compelled to say "How long, O Lord?"

Farewell,

C. S. LEWIS

10

Casa Buoni Fanciulli
Verona

Easter, the Passion of the Lord, 1949
17th April 1949

Most beloved in Christ,

May the grace and peace of Christ exult in your heart. The appointed days draw near in which we celebrate the Resurrection of the Lord Jesus. My thoughts are daily towards you and especially in these days of prayerful good wishes for brothers and friends.

May the Lord Jesus give you His peace with the kiss of love. May He help you to multiply your good works in bringing on the young people committed to your care so that in their acquisition of human learning you may promote in them heavenly aspirations. On you and on your household may the sun of joy, and of cheerfulness in the Lord, continually shine; so that in this transitory life you may spend virtuous and prosperous days; and, at the end, in His time prove fit to enter the Paradise of eternal felicity with the fruits of your good works.

Such are my prayers in this our Paschal season.

quaeramus sincere. Utinam omnes audiamus hanc Patris vocem, et tandem aliquando ad Dominum convertamur! Det nobis Dominus Jesus ut his diebus suae Resurrectionis – post Passionem et Mortem pro nobis – adlaborare possimus ut familia humana resurgat in novitate vitae Christi et Domini.

Vale! et semper mei memoriam apud Deum feceris in precibus: misericordia Domini indigeo! Ego tui semper, cotidie, memor sum in meis precibus. Diligamus invicem nuns, ut invicem gaudeamus in Caelo.

Ad pedes Crucifixi dictavi hanc litteram.

Leges in corde meo omnia quae dicere voluissem tibi si valetudo permisisset.

[Phrases retro scriptae]

11

E Collegio Stae Mariae Magdalenensis
apud Oxonios

Sept. x° A. D. mdccccxlix

Dilecte Pater, nuper in scriniis meis inveni epistolam tuam quam benevolo animo scripsisti Paschâ praesentis anni. Credo me nullum responsum misisse: quo silentio meo nihil minus civile, minus humanum, fieri potuit. Culpam agnosco, veniam peto. Nolo autem te credere aut memoriam tui ex animo aut nomen tuum ex orationibus meis quotidianis excidisse. Nihil enim aliud in causa erat nisi perpetuus scribendi labor necnon (ne nimis me exculpare videar) accidia quaedam – mala pestis et (credo) VII

May good times come! The voice of God indeed daily calls to us; calls to the world to abandon sins and seek the Kingdom of God wholeheartedly. O that we may all hear the call of the Father and, sometime, at last be converted to the Lord. May the Lord Jesus grant that in these days of His Resurrection – after His passion and Death for us – we be able to assist the human family to be raised up in the newness of life of Christ our Lord.

Farewell! And may you ever make remembrance of me in your prayers: I need God's mercy! In my prayers I ever daily remember you.

At the foot of the Crucified One I have composed this letter. You will read in my heart all that I would have said to you had health permitted.

[Some writing on the back]

11

from the College of St Mary Magdalen
Oxford

10th September in the year of Our Lord 1949

Dear Father,

I have just found in my desk the letter which you so kindly wrote at Easter this year. I think I have sent no reply: nothing could be less civil than this silence of mine, nothing less human. I acknowledge my fault, I ask pardon. But I do not wish you to believe either that your memory has fallen from my mind or that your name has fallen from my daily prayers. For nothing else was responsible for it except the perpetual labour of writing and (lest

istorum mortalium vitiorum in me validissimum, quamquam hoc de me pauci credunt.

Ex brevi valetudine, Deo gratia, sanatus sum. Passus sum morbum quem medici olim *tonsilitim* anglice appellabant nunc vero splendidiore titulo *streptococcum.* Febris haud modica incumbebat et horas quasdam deliravi . . . o quam bene poeta vester scripsit de animis perditis qui *han perduto it ben dell intell'et-to:* quid enim supplicium atrocius? Nam dum mens alienatur nobismet videmur multo cogitationis negotio laborare syllogismos contexere, quaestiones subtilissimas tractare, nescientes tamen quid sit de quo cogitamus. Operatio mentis adest, opus abest.

In hac insula gravis carentia imbris nos vexat. De aliis nationibus taceo. Quid enim ad me nisi ut magis magisque teneam infixa cordi Dominica verba "Audituri estis praelia et opiniones praeliorum. Videte ne turbemini"?

Vale, mi pater, nec cesses ex paterna caritate apud communem Dominum (verum Deum et solum verum Hominem, ceteri enim nos omnes, post Adami lapsum, semihomines) mentionem mei facere

vester,

C. S. LEWIS

I should seem to exonerate myself too much) a certain Accidia, an evil disease and, I believe, of the Seven Deadly Sins that one which in me is the strongest – though few believe this of me.

From a brief illness, God be thanked, I am recovered. I had what the doctors once used to call in English "tonsilitis": but now by a more splendid name, "streptococcus". Fever laid on me a heavy hand and for some hours I was delirious . . . O how well has your poet written of the lost souls who "have lost the good of the intellect": for what torture is more dreadful than that? For while the mind is alienated from us, to ourselves we seem to toil away with much effort of thought, to knit together syllogisms, to treat of the most subtle questions – not knowing, however, what it is we are thinking about. The *working* of the mind is there, but not its *work*.

In this island we are troubled by a severe drought. About other nations I say nothing. For what is required of me unless more and more to hold fixed in my heart our Lord's words:

"Ye shall hear of wars and rumours of wars. See that ye be not troubled"?

Farewell, my Father; and of your fatherly charity cease not to make mention of me before our common Lord (true God and the only true Man – for all we others, since the Fall of Adam, are but half men).

Yours,
C. S. LEWIS

12

Lettera del Padre D. Giovanni Calabria
al Prof. C. S. Lewis
Verona

18 sett. '49

Dilectissime in Domino,

Gratia tibi, pax a Deo nostro Christo Jesu, qui nos in partem sanctorum vocavit.

Pergratum mihi fuit solamen ex tuis litteris, quas nuper accepi. Ego valde cupiebam aliquod tui nuntium recipere post plures menses a tua epistola; timebam ne salus tua defecisset. Nunc Deo gratias ago de recuperata valetudine tua; et divinam benignitatem rogo ut tibi multos annos concedat quibus adlaborare possis ad Dei gloriam et fratrum salutem.

Ego semper tui memor sum; pro certo mihi videris vocatus ad missionem specialem in bonum proximi; hac hora, his temporibus difficilimis, divina Providentia poscit a nobis ut caritate compulsi Evangelium portemus manifeste, in vita nostra cotidiana, ita ut ceteri "videant opera nostra et glorificent Patrem".

Dona mentis et cordis, quibus polles, locum quem tenes coram juvenibus studio addictis, satis perspicua sunt signa divinae erga te voluntatis. Deus a te exspectat ut verbo et opere fratres adducas fortiter et suaviter ad Evangelium Christi.

Pulchre to dicis nos semihomines esse, quia pleni miseriis et peccatis. Sed habemus Pontificem qui condolere potest, et dare nobis sufficientiam ad opus commissum explendum. Non quod simus validi ex nostris viribus; sed "sufficientia nostra ex Deo est".

Eja ergo, adlaboremus corde generoso, fide intrepida ad regnum Dei dilatandum, ad fratres nostros complectendos unitate fidei et dilectionis, ad pugnandum quam strenue ut amor Christi

12

Letter from Father D. John Calabria to
Prof. C. S. Lewis
Verona

18th September 1949

Most beloved in the Lord,

Grace to you and peace from God and our Lord Jesus Christ who has called us into the portion of His Saints.

The consolation from your letter, which I have lately received, was most welcome to me. For many months after your letter I longed to receive some news of you; I was afraid lest your health had failed. Now I give thanks to God for your restoration to strength; and I pray the goodness of God that He will grant you many years in which you may be able to work to the glory of God and the salvation of the brethren.

I always have you in mind; certainly you seem to me to be called to a special mission for the good of your neighbour; at this hour, in these difficult times, Divine Providence demands from us that, compelled by love, we openly carry the Gospel in our daily life so that others may "see our works and glorify the Father". The gifts of mind and heart which are your strength, the place which you hold among young students, are sufficiently clear signs of God's will in respect of yourself. God expects from you that by word and deed you will firmly and gently bring brethren to the Gospel of Christ.

Well do you say that we are half-men because we are full of miseries and sins. But we have a High Priest who is able to suffer with us and give us sufficient strength to carry out the tasks committed to us. Not that we are strong with our own strength; "but our sufficiency is of God".

Then, let us work – with a generous heart and with an intrepid

vincat, regnet et imperet in mundo universo. Sine Eo nihil possumus; sed "omnia possumus in Eo, qui nos confortat".

Haec anima recolo, dum coram Crucifixo de te recognito, et pro te preces effundo ut dignus magis magisque habearis miles Christi Jesu. Et tu memor sis mei, qui ad occasum vitae festino, ut Dei miseratione dignus inveniar et locum refrigerii ingrediar.

Semper in caritate Christi et Dei conjunctos nos invicem sentiamus in terris; et in gaudio caelesti comparticipes nos faciat Deus bonus et clemens.

13

Magdalen College
Oxford

19th November 1949

Dilectissime Pater,

Remitto ad te epistolam hodie acceptam in qua et oculos meos (jam admodum debiles) et parvam meam vestri vernaculi sermonis peritiam superavit chirographiae difficultas. Ne nomen quidem viri possum legere; sententiarum *disjecta membra* modo intellexi! Hanc chartam (Sibyllinum librum!) tibi remitto ne auctor, vir procul dubio plenus caritate, credat me inhumaniter neglexisse. Si Anglice vel Latine manu scripserit aut si Italice dactylographica machina usus fuerit communicatio intra nos fieri

faith for the spread of God's Kingdom – to clasp our brothers together in the unity of faith and love, striving as strenuously as possible to bring it about that Christ's love may conquer, reign and rule in the whole world. Without Him, we can do nothing: but we "can do all things in Him who strengthens" us.

These things I bear in mind when I think of you again in the presence of the Crucified One; and I pour out prayers for you that you may more and more be regarded as a worthy soldier of Christ Jesus. And do you remember me who am hastening to the end of life, that I may be found worthy of the mercy of God and that I may come to a place of refreshment.

May we always feel ourselves bound one to another on earth in the love of Christ and of God; and may God, the Good and the Merciful, make us sharers in the joy of Heaven.

13

Magdalen College
Oxford

19th November 1949

Dearest Father,

I send back to you a letter which I received today in which the difficulty of the handwriting was too much both for my eyesight – my eyes are now rather weak – and for my limited experience of your language. I cannot even read the name of the writer: I can scarcely understand the "scattered limbs" of his sentences. I send you back this letter (a Sibylline book!) lest the writer, a man without doubt full of charity, should think that I have discourteously neglected him.

poterit. Interea et scriptori et tibi mitto fraternas aut filiales salutationes illas praesertim quae ad hoc beatum tempus pertinent quo nos iterum Bethlehem petimus et Sanctum Infantem; quem oremus ut nos, aetate et longa consuetudine peccandi confectos novos homines reddat et ducat in regnum suum ubi nisi sub specie infantis nullus introitus est. Gaudeo quia Dominus qui ceteras miserias nostras omnes suscepit non voluit senilitatem suscipere; in Uno Vero Homine aeterna juventus. Valete et tu et ignotus ille scriptor.

C. S. LEWIS

14

Verona

17 dec. '49

Dilectissime in Christo,

Gratia tibi et pax, quae exsuperat omnem sensum et ab Angelo nuntiata est Bethlem.

Proximae sunt celebritates Natalis D.N. JESU Ch. et ego, hic sedens coram Crucifixo, recogito fratres et amicos, quos divina Providentia invenire me fecit. Te recogito, dilectissime frater, quocum vinculo arcto et dulci me sentio conjunctum ex quo epistolis nos cognovimus.

Gratias et dona tibi invoco a Puero Jesu in hac sacra sollemnitate Natalis; omnia quae cor tuum optat concedat tibi Deus

If he will write in English or in Latin, or if in Italian he will use a typewriter, communication between us will be possible.

Meanwhile both to the writer and to you I send greetings fraternal and filial respectively, especially those greetings which belong to this blessed time wherein we again seek Bethlehem and the Holy Child. Let us pray to Him that, weakened as we are by age and the long habit of sinning, He may make new persons of us and lead us into His Kingdom – that Kingdom into which there is no entry except in the likeness of a child. I rejoice that the Lord, who took upon Him all our other miseries, willed not to take old age: in the One True Man, lives youth everlasting.

Farewell, both to you and to the unknown writer,

C. S. LEWIS

14

Verona

17th December 1949

Most beloved in Christ,

Grace to you and the peace which exceeds all knowledge and was announced by the angel at Bethlehem.

We are approaching the celebrations of the Birth of Our Lord Jesus Christ and I, sitting here in front of the Crucified One, remember my brothers and friends whom Divine Providence has caused me to find. I think of you, my dearest brother, with whom ever since we made each other's acquaintance by letters, I feel myself joined by a close, sweet bond.

I invoke for you graces and gifts from the Child Jesus in this

omnipotens de sua miseratione. Et tuis omnibus det pacem et salutem, gaudium de corde puro atque perfecto, amorem et dilectionem sui.

Infans Jesus, repositus in praesepio, mihi videtur oculis ac manibus adhuc parvulis dicere hominibus omnibus: "Venite ad me, omnes; volo ut omnes unum sint . . ." Annus Sanctus Jubilei maximi, in quem intramus, sit annus pacis in caritate et unitate cordium!

Oremus ad invicem, ut desiderium Christi adimpleatur quam primum; et omnes de christiana familia adlaboremus ut fratres "habitent in unum"; omnes in novitate vitae ambulemus, ita ut ceteros omnes, qui vel ob neglegentiam vel praejudicatasque opiniones aberrarunt, praelucenti exemplo vitae attrahamus ad ovile Christi, ad bonam frugem.

Haec anima meo recogito; haec vota mea, quae etiam tua sunt.

Vale, dilectissime frater; et pro me Deum exora.

15

Magdalen College
Oxford

13th September 1951

Dilectissime Pater,

Insolito gaudio affectus sum tuâ epistolâ et eo magis quod audivi te aegritudine laborare; interdum timui ne forte mortem obisses. Minime tamen cessavi ab orationibus pro te: neque enim

sacred solemnity of His Birth; may Almighty God in His mercy grant you all that your heart desires. And to all yours may He give peace and salvation, joy from a pure and perfect heart, and His love and favour.

The infant Jesus, resting in the crib, seems to me to be saying to all men with his eyes and his still tiny hands, "Come to Me all of you; I wish that you all be one". May the Holy Year of supreme Jubilee upon which we are entering be a year of peace in the love and unity of hearts!

Let us pray for one another that the longing of Christ may be fulfilled as soon as possible; and let all of us from the Christian family labour to bring it about that brethren "dwell together in unity". Let us all walk in newness of life, so that, by the light of our life's example, we may draw to the flock of Christ, and to yielding good fruit, all those others who, through either negligence or prejudiced opinions, have strayed from the way.

These are the thoughts which I turn over in my mind. These are my prayers which also are yours.

Farewell, dearest brother, and pray to God for me.

15

Magdalen College
Oxford

13th September 1951

Dearest Father,

I was moved with unaccustomed joy by your letter and all the more because I had heard you were ill; sometimes I feared lest you had perhaps died.

debet illud Flumen Mortis dulce commercium caritatis et cogita-
tionum abolere. Nunc gaudeo quia credo (quamquam taces de
valetudine – noli contemnere corpus, Fratrem Asinum, ut dixit
Sanctus Franciscus!) tibi iam bene aut saltem melius esse. Mitto
ad te fabulam meam nuper Italice versam; in qua sane magis lusi
quam laboravi. Fantasiae meae liberas remisi habenas haud
tamen (spero) sine respectu ad aedificationem et meam et proximi. Nescio utrum hujusmodi nugis dilecteris; at si non tu, fortasse
quidam juvenis aut puella ex *bonis* tuis *liberis* amabit. Equidem
post longam successionem modicorum morborum (quorum nomina Italica nescio) iam valeo. Quinquagesimum diem natalem sacerdotii tui gratulationibus, precibus, benedictionibus saluto. Vale.
Oremus pro invicem semper in hoc mundo et in futuro.

C. S. LEWIS

16

e Collegio S. Mariae Magdalenae
apud Oxonienses

Die S. Stephani MCMLI (26th December 1951)

Dilectissime Pater,

Grato animo epistulam tuam hodie accepi et omnia bona
spiritualia et temporalia tibi in Domino invoco. Mihi in praeteri-
to anno accidit magnum gaudium quod quamquam difficile est
verbis exprimere conabor.

But never in the least did I cease from my prayers for you; for not even the River of Death ought to abolish the sweet intercourse of love and meditations.

Now I rejoice because I believe (although you keep silent about your health – do not condemn the body: Brother Ass, as St Francis said!) I believe you are well or at least better.

I am sending you my tale recently translated into Italian in which, frankly, I have rather played than worked. I have given my imagination free rein yet not, I hope, without regard for edifi-cation – for building up both my neighbour and myself.

I do not know whether you will like this kind of trifle. But if you do not, perhaps some boy or girl will like it from among your "good children".

For myself, after a long succession of minor illnesses (I do not know their Italian names) I am now better.

I salute the fiftieth anniversary of your priesthood with con-gratulations, prayers and blessings.

Farewell. May we always pray for one another both in this world and in the world to come.

C. S. LEWIS

16

from the College of St Mary Magdalen
Oxford

26th December
St Stephen's Day, 1951

Dearest Father,

Thank you for the letter which I have received from you today and I invoke upon you all spiritual and temporal blessings in the Lord.

Mirum est quod interdum credimus nos credere quae re verâ ex corde non credimus. Diu credebam me credere in remissionem peccatorum. Ac subito (in die S. Marci) haec veritas in mente mea tarn manifesto lumine apparuit ut perciperem me numquam antea (etiam post multas confessiones et absolutiones) toto corde hoc credidisse. Tantum distat inter intellectûs meram affirmationem et illa fides medullitus infixa et quasi palpabilis quam apostolus scripsit esse *substantiam*.

Fortasse haec liberatio concessa est tuis pro me intercessionibus! Confortat me ad dicendum tibi quod vix debet laicus ad sacerdotem, junior ad seniorem, dicere. (Attamen *ex ore infantium:* immo olim ad Balaam ex ore asini!). Hoc est: multum scribis de tuis peccatis. Cave (liceat mihi, dilectissime pater, dicere *cave)* ne humilitas in anxietatem aut tristitiam transeat. Mandatum est *gaude* et *semper gaude.* Jesus abolevit chirographiam quae contra nos erat. Sursum corda! Indulge mihi, precor, has balbutiones. Semper in meis orationibus et es et eris. Vale.

C S. LEWIS

As for myself, during the past year a great joy has befallen me. Difficult though it is, I shall try to explain this in words.

It is astonishing that sometimes we believe that we believe what, really, in our heart, we do not believe.

For a long time I believed that I believed in the forgiveness of sins. But suddenly (on St Mark's day) this truth appeared in my mind in so clear a light that I perceived that never before (and that after many confessions and absolutions) had I believed it with my whole heart.

So great is the difference between mere affirmation by the intellect and that faith, fixed in the very marrow and as it were palpable, which the Apostle wrote was *substance.*

Perhaps I was granted this deliverance in response to your intercessions on my behalf!

This emboldens me to say to you something that a layman ought scarcely to say to a priest nor a junior to a senior. (On the other hand, *out of the mouths of babes:* indeed, as once to Balaam, out of the mouth of an ass!)

It is this: you write much about your own sins. Beware (permit me, my dearest Father, to say beware) lest humility should pass over into anxiety or sadness. It is bidden us to "rejoice and always rejoice". Jesus has cancelled the handwriting which was against us. Lift up our hearts!

Permit me, I pray you, these stammerings. You are ever in my prayers and ever will be.

Farewell.

C. S. LEWIS

17

Magdalen College
Oxford

14th April 1952

Pater dilectissime,

Multum eras et es in orationibus meis et grato animo litteras tuas accepi. Et ora tu pro me, nunc praesertim, dum me admodum orphanum esse sentio quia grandaevus meus confessor et carissimus pater in Christo nuper mortem obiit. Dum ad altare celebraret, subito, post acerrimum sed (Deo gratias) brevissimum dolorem, expiravit, et novissima verba erant *venio, Domine Jesu.* Vir erat maturâ spirituali sapientiâ sed ingenuitate et innocentiâ fere puerili – *buono fanciullo,* ut ita dicam.

Potesne, mi pater, quaestionem resolvere? Quis sanctorum scriptorum scripsit "Amor est ignis jugiter ardens" ? Credidi haec verba esse in libro *De Imitatione Christi* sed non possum ibi invenire.

"Ut omnes unum sint" est petitio numquam in meis precibus praetermissa. Dum optabilis unitas doctrinae et ordinis abest, eo acrius conemur caritatis unionem tenere: quod, eheu, et vestri in Hispania et nostri in Hibernia Septentrionali non faciunt.

Vale, mi pater,

C. S. LEWIS

17

Magdalen College
Oxford

14th April 1952

Dearest Father,

You were and are much in my prayers and thank you for your letters. And do you pray for me, especially at present when I feel very much an orphan because my aged confessor and most loving father in Christ has just died. While he was celebrating at the altar, suddenly, after a most sharp but (thanks be to God) very brief attack of pain, he expired; and his last words were, "I come, Lord Jesus". He was a man of ripe spiritual wisdom – noble minded but of an almost childlike simplicity and innocence: "buono fanciullo", if I may put it so.

Can you, my Father, resolve a question? Which of the holy writers wrote *"Amor est ignis jugiter ardens"*?* I thought these words were in *The Imitation of Christ* but I cannot find them there.

"That they all may be one" is a petition which in my prayers I never omit. While the wished-for unity of doctrine and order is missing, all the more eagerly let us try to keep the bond of charity: which, alas, your people in Spain and ours in Northern Ireland do not.

Farewell, my Father.

C. S. LEWIS

* Love is a fire continually burning *(Imitation,* Book 4, Chapter 4).

18

e Coll. Stae Mariae Magdalenae

Jul. XIV MCMLII

Gratias ago, dilectissime pater, et pro opusculis Congregationis vestrae et pro hac epistolâ Jul vii datâ. Hora nostra, ut dicis, gravis est: utrum gravis "prae omnibus humanae historiae" nescio. Sed semper malum quod proximum et gravissimum videtur esse; est enim, ut oculis, sic cordibus, sua "perspettiva". Si tamen nostra tempestas rê verâ pessima est, si rêverâ Dies Illa nunc imminet, quid restat nisi ut gaudeamus quia redemptio nostra iam propior est et dicamus cum Sancto Joanne "Amen; cito venias, domine Iesu" Interim sola securitas est ut Dies nos inveniat laborantes quemque in suo officio et praecipue (dissensionibus relictis) illud supremum mandatum ut invicem diligamus implentes. Oremus semper pro invicem. Vale: et sit tecum et mecum pax illa quam nemo potest auferre.

C. S. LEWIS

18

from the College of St Mary Magdalen

14th July 1952

Thank you, dearest Father, both for the tracts of your Congregation and for your letter dated July 7th.

The times we live in are, as you say, grave: whether "graver than all others in history" I do not know. But the evil that is closest always seems to be the most serious: for as with the eye so with the heart, it is a matter of one's own perspective. However, if our times are indeed the worst, if That Day is indeed now approaching, what remains but that we should rejoice because our redemption is now nearer and say with St John: "Amen; come quickly, Lord Jesus."

Meanwhile our only security is that The Day may find us working each one in his own station and especially (giving up dissensions) fulfilling that supreme command that we love one another.

Let us ever pray for each other.

Farewell: and may there abide with you and me that peace which no one can take from us.

C. S. LEWIS

19

Collegium Stae Mariae Magdalenae
apud Oxonienses

Vig. fest. Trium Regum
MCMLIII
5 Jan. 1953

Dilectissme Pater,

Grato animo, ut semper, paternas tuas benedictiones accepi. Sit tibi, precor, suavissima gustatio omnium hujus temporis gaudiorum et inter curas et dolores consolatio. Tractatum *Responsabilità* apud *Amicum* (Dec.) invenire nequeo. Latet aliquis error. Orationes tuas peto de opere quod nunc in manibus est dum conor componere libellum de precibus privatis in usum laicorum praesertim eorum qui nuper in fidem Christianam conversi sunt et longo stabilitoque habitu orandi adhuc carent. Laborem aggressus sum quia videbam multos quidem pulcherrimosque libros de hac re scriptos esse in usum religiosorum, paucos tamen qui tirones et adhuc (ut ita dicam) infantes in fide instruunt. Multas difficultates invenio nec certe scio utrum Dominus velit me hoc opus perficere an non. Ora, mi pater, ne aut nimia audacitate in re mihi non concessâ persistam aut nimia timiditate a labore debito recedam: aeque enim damnati et ille qui Arcam sine mandato tetigit et ille qui manum semel aratro impositam abstrahit.

Et tu et congregatio tua in diurnis orationibus meis. Haec sola, dum in via sumus, conversatio: liceat nobis, precor, olim in Patria facie ad faciem congredi. Vale.

C. S. LEWIS

Adhuc spero tractatum *Responsabilità* accipere.

19

The College of St Mary Magdalen
Oxford

Vigil of the Feast of the Three Kings, 1953
(5th January 1953)

Dearest Father,

Thank you, as always, for your fatherly blessings.

May you, I pray, have the sweetest relish of all the joys of this life and consolation amid cares and griefs.

I am unable to find the article "Responsibility" in the December issue of *Friend.* There is some unexplained mistake here.

I invite your prayers about a work which I now have in hand. I am trying to write a book about private prayers for the use of the laity, especially for those who have been recently converted to the Christian faith and so far are without any sustained and regular habit of prayer. I tackled the job because I saw many no doubt very beautiful books written on this subject of prayer for the religious but few which instruct tiros and those still babes (so to say) in the Faith. I find many difficulties nor do I definitely know whether God wishes me to complete this task or not.

Pray for me, my Father, that I neither persist, through over-boldness, in what is not permitted to me nor withdraw, through too great timidity, from due effort: for he who touches the Ark without authorization and he who, having once put his hand to the plough, draws it back are both lost.

Both you and your Congregation are in my daily prayers. While we are in the Way, this is our only intercourse: be it granted to us, I pray, hereafter, to meet in our True Country face to face.

C. S. LEWIS

I still hope to receive the article "Responsibility".

20

Tandem, pater dilectissime, venit in manus exemplar *Amici (Oct.)* quod continet tractatum tuum de clade illa Serica. De illa natione quum ibi per multos annos evangelistae haud infeliciter laboravissent, equidem multa sperabam: nunc omnia retro fluere, ut scribis, manifestum est. Et mihi multa atrocia multi de illa re epistolis renuntiaverunt neque aberat ista miseria a cogitationibus et precibus nostris. Neque tamen sine peccatis nostris evenit: nos enim justitiam illam, curam illam pauperum quas (mendacissime) communistae praeferunt debueramus jam ante multa saecula rê verâ effecisse. Sed longe hoc aberat: nos occidentales Christum ore praedicavimus, factis Mammoni servitium tulimus. Magis culpabiles nos quam infideles: scientibus enim voluntatem Dei et non facientibus major poena. Nunc unicum refugium in contritione et oratione. Diu erravimus. In legendo Europae historiam, seriem exitiabilem bellorum, avaritiae, fratricidarum Christianorum a Christianis persecutionum, luxuriae, gulae, superbiae, quis discerneret rarissima Sancti Spiritus vestigia? Oremus semper. Vale.

C. S. LEWIS

20

At last, dearest Father, there has come to hand that copy of *Friend (Oct.)* which contains your article on that Chinese disaster. I used myself to entertain many hopes for that nation, since the missionaries have served there for many years not unsuccessfully: now it is clear, as you write, that all is on the ebb. Many have reported to me too, in letters on this subject, many atrocities, nor was this misery absent from our thoughts and prayers.

But it did not happen, however, without sins on our part: for that justice and that care for the poor which (most mendaciously) the Communists advertise, we in reality ought to have brought about ages ago. But far from it: we Westerners preached Christ with our lips, with our actions we brought the slavery of Mammon. We are more guilty than the infidels: for to those that know the will of God and do it not, the greater the punishment.

Now the only refuge lies in contrition and prayer. Long have we erred. In reading the history of Europe, its destructive succession of wars, of avarice, or fratricidal persecutions of Christians by Christians, of luxury, of gluttony, of pride, who could detect any but the rarest traces of the Holy Spirit?

Let us pray always. Farewell,

C. S. LEWIS

21

Siamo in giorni santi, i più santi auguri a Lei che (dalla) Div.
Prov. (siamo uniti nel) vincolo (di una) completa carità fraterna.
(La) ricordo (nelle) mie preghiere e sofferenze, perchè il Signore
compia anche per la sua alta missione e per i doni che Gesù (Le)
ha dato, it bene in quest'ora, per chiamare anime al Vangelo. Il
Signore La benedica, Le doni ogni bene anche ai suoi cari. Son
certo della carità grande (delle) sue preghiere ne ho grande bisog-
no per me e per l'Opera dei Poveri Servi, per fare fino in fondo la
divina volonta. Ruit hora. Che tutti quanti, terminato il tempo,
possiamo trovarci nella (eterna) felicità. Non so se Le hanno man-
data questo fascicolo con l'articolo del Rev. Padre Manna che
tanto mi sta a cuore.

21

Verona

((?) 9th January 1953)

We are in holy days. The most sacred blessings to you, that by Divine Providence we are united in the bond of full brotherly charity. I remember you in my prayers and sufferings, that the Lord may at this time fulfil His goodness both through His high mission and through the gifts that Jesus has bestowed on you, to summon souls to the Gospel.

May the Lord bless you, and grant every good thing to you as well as to His dear ones. I am assured of the great love of your prayers – of which I have great need for myself and for the work of the Poor Servants – that I may carry out the divine will even to the end. Time presses *(Ruit Nora)* . May He grant that in the fulfilment of time we may all find ourselves in His everlasting happiness.

I do not know if they have sent you this copy with the article of Rev. Father Manna which is so close to my heart.

22

E Coll. Stae Mariae Magdalenae
apud Oxonienses

Jan. (? Jun.) xiv LIII

Pater dilectissime,

Multo gaudio accepi epistolam tuam die ix Jan. (? Jun.) datam: credo jampridem te meam accepisse quam de tractatu *Responsabilità* scripsi. Et vides me per errorem putavisse te auctorem esse et Sac. P. Mannam esse id quod Galli vocant nomen plumae. At minime refert quum liber *De Imitatione* nos doceat "Attende quid dicatur, non quis dixerit". Multas ex corde gratias refero, quia tanta caritate ob libellum meum propositum meditare et orare voluisti. Sententiam tuam pro signo accipio. Et nunc, carissime, audi de quâ difficultate maxime haesito. Duo paradigmata orationis videntur nobis in Novo Testamento exposita esse quae inter se conciliare haud facile est. Alterum est ipsa Domini oratio in horto Gethsemane ("si possibile est . . . nihilominus non quod ego volo sed quod tu vis"). Alterum vero apud Marc XI, v. 24 "Quidquid petieritis credentes quod accipietis, habebitis". (Et nota, loco quo versio latina *accipietis* habet et nostra vernacula similiter futurum tempus *shall receive,* graecus textus tempus praeteritum ἐλάβετε, accepistis, id quod dificillimum est). Nunc quaestio: quomodo potest homo uno eodemque momento temporis et credere plenissime se accepturum et voluntati Dei fortasse negantis se submittere? Quomodo potest dicere simul "Credo firmiter te hoc daturum esse" et "si hoc negaveris, fiat voluntas tua". Quomodo potest unus actus mentis et possibilem negationem excludere et tractare? Rem a nullo doctorum tractatam invenio.

Nota bene: nullam difficultatem mihi facit quod Deus interdum non vult facere ea quae fideles petunt. Necesse est quippe

22

14th January (? June) 1953

Dearest Father,

I received your letter dated 9th Jan. with much joy. I trust that long since you have received my letter on the tract *Responsabilità*.

And you see that I mistakenly thought that you yourself were the author and that *"Sac. P. Mannam"* was what the French call a *nom de plume*.

But it is of no consequence since the *De Imitatione* teaches us to "Mark *what* is said, not *who* said it".

I send you many heartfelt thanks for your charity in being willing to meditate on my proposed little book and pray for it. I take your opinion as a good sign.

And now, my dearest friend, hear what difficulty leaves me in most doubt. Two models of prayer seem to be put before us in the New Testament which are not easy to reconcile with each other.

One is the actual prayer of the Lord in the Garden of Gethsemane ("if it be possible . . . nevertheless, not as I will but as Thou wilt").

The other, though, is in Mark XI v. 24. "Whatsoever you ask believing that you shall receive you shall obtain" (and observe that in the place where the version has, in Latin, *accipietis* – and our vernacular translation, similarly, has the *future* tense, "shall receive" – the Greek text has the *past* tense ἐλάβετε = *accepistis* – which is very difficult).

Now the question: How is it possible for a man, at one and the same moment of time, *both* to believe most fully that he *will* receive *and* to submit himself to the Will of God – Who perhaps is refusing him?

ille sapiens et nos stulti sed cur apud Marc. XI 24 pollicetur se omnia *(quidquid)* facere quas plena fide petimus? Ambo loci Dominici, ambo inter credenda. Quid faciam? Vale. Et pro te et pro congregatione tua oro et semper orabo.

C. S. LEWIS

23

Magdalen College
Oxford

Mart. xvii MCMLIII

Dilectissime Pater,

Gavisus sum, ut semper, de epistola tua. Res mira est et corroboratio fidei duas animas loco, natione, lingua, oboedentia, aetate diversas sic in dulcem familiaritatem adductas esse; adeo ordo spirituum ordinem materialem superat. Reddit faciliorem illam necessariam doctrinam, nos arctissime conjungi et cum peccatore Adamo et cum justo Jesu quamquam (secundum carnem,

How is it possible to say, simultaneously, "I firmly believe that Thou wilt give me this", *and,* "If Thou shalt deny me it, Thy will be done"? How can one mental act both exclude possible refusal and consider it? I find this discussed by none of the Doctors.

Please note: it creates no difficulty for me that God sometimes does not will to do what the faithful request. This is necessary because He is wise and we are foolish: but why in Mark XI 24, does He promise to do everything (whatsoever) we ask in full faith? Both statements are the Lord's; both are among what we are required to believe. What should I do?

Farewell. And for you and for your Congregation I pray and shall ever pray.

C. S. LEWIS

23

Magdalen College

Oxford

17th March 1953

My dearest Father,

I was delighted, as always, by your letter.

It is a wonderful thing and a strengthening of faith that two souls differing from each other in place, nationality, language, obedience and age should have been thus led into a delightful friendship; so far does the order of spiritual beings transcend the material order.

It makes easier that necessary doctrine that we are most closely

tempus et locum) tam diversi ab ambobus viximus. Haec unitas totius humani generis extat: utinam extaret praestantior illa unio de quo scribis. Nullum diem sine oratione pro illo optato fine praetereo. Quae dicis de praesenti statu hominum vera sunt: immo deterior est quam dicis. Non enim Christi modo legem sed etiam legem Naturae Paganis cognitam negligunt. Nunc enim non erubescunt de adulterio, proditione, perjurio, furto, ceterisque flagitiis quae non dico Christianos doctores, sed ipsi pagani et barbari reprobaverunt. Falluntur qui dicunt "Mundus iterum Paganus fit" Utinam fieret! Re vera in statum multo pejorem cadimus. Homo *post-Christianus* non similis homini *pre-Christiano*. Tantum distant ut vidua a virgine: nihil commune est nisi absentia sponsi: sed magna differentia intra absentiam sponsi venturi et sponsi amissi! Adhuc laboro in libro de oratione. De hac quaestione quam tibi subjeci, omnes theologos interrogo: adhuc frustra.

Oremus semper pro invicem, mi pater. Vale,

C. S. LEWIS

joined together alike with the sinner Adam and with the Just One, Jesus, even though as to body, time and place we have lived so differently from both. This unity of the whole human race exists: would that there existed that nobler union of which you write. No day do I let pass without my praying for that longed-for consummation.

What you say about the present state of mankind is true: indeed, it is even worse than you say.

For they neglect not only the law of Christ but even the Law of Nature as known by the Pagans. For now they do not blush at adultery, treachery, perjury, theft and the other crimes which I will not say Christian Doctors, but the Pagans and the Barbarians have themselves denounced.

They err who say "the world is turning pagan again". Would that it were! The truth is that we are falling into a much worse state.

"Post-Christian man" is not the same as "pre-Christian man". He is as far removed as virgin is from widow: there is nothing in common except want of a spouse: but there is a great difference between a spouse-to-come and a spouse lost.

I am still working on my book on Prayer.

About this question which I submitted to you, I am asking all theologians: so far in vain.

Let us ever pray for each other, my Father.

Farewell,

C. S. LEWIS

24

Collegium Stae Mariae
Magdalenae apud
Oxonienses

Aug. x. MCMLIII

Dilectissime Pater, Accepi litteras tuas V^{to} Augusti datas. Expecto cum gratiarum actione opuscula, specimen artis vestrae typographicae: quae tamen non videbo nisi post V hebdomadas quia pertransibo cras (si Deo placuerit) in Hiberniam; incunabula mea et dulcissimum refugium, quoad amoenitatem locorum et caeli temperiem quamquam rixis et odiis et saepe civilibus armis dissentientium religionum atrocissimam. Ibi sane et vestri et nostri "ignorant quo spiritu ducantur": carentiam caritatis pro zelo accipiunt et reciprocam ignorantiam pro orthodoxia. Puto fere omnia facinora quae invicem perpetraverunt Christiani ex illo evenerunt quod religio miscetur cum re politica. Diabolus enim supra omnes ceteras humanas vitae partes rem politicam sibi quasi propriam – quasi arcem suae potestatis – vindicat. Nos tamen pro viribus (sc. quisque) suis mutuis orationibus incessanter laboremus pro caritate quae "multitudinem peccatorum tegit." Vale, sodes et pater.

C. S. LEWIS

24

The College of St Mary Magdalen
Oxford

10th August 1953

Dearest Father,

I have received your letter dated the 5th August. I await with gratitude the pamphlets – a specimen of your people's printing skill: which however I shall not see for 5 weeks because tomorrow I am crossing over (if God so have pleased) to Ireland: my birthplace and dearest refuge so far as charm of landscape goes, and temperate climate, although most dreadful because of the strife, hatred and often civil war between dissenting faiths.

There indeed both yours and ours "know not by what Spirit they are led". They take lack of charity for zeal and mutual ignorance for orthodoxy.

I think almost all the crimes which Christians have perpetrated against each other arise from this, that religion is confused with politics. For, above all other spheres of human life, the Devil claims politics for his own, as almost the citadel of his power. Let us, however, with mutual prayers pray with all our power for that charity which "covers a multitude of sins". Farewell, comrade and father.

C. S. LEWIS

25

Verona

3 settembre 1953

Dilectissime in Christo,

Gratia et pax multiplicentur tibi tuisque.

His diebus ego, una cum muftis fratribus huius Congregationis Pauperum Servorum div. Providentiae, exercitiis spiritualibus vaco; sunt enim Exercitia ad reformandos mores, ad perfectionem adipiscendam, ad vitam religiosam renovandam. In silentio et in meditatione aeternarum veritatum, audio vocem Dei, quae ad majorem caritatem cor nostrum excitat. Ora, frater dilectissime, ut non in vacuum gratiam Dei recipiam; sed in timore et gaudio gratiam Dei recipiam et superlucrari valeam.

Dum autem Deo attendo et animae meae, te recogito peculiarissimo modo his diebus gratiae et veritatis; tua verba praesertim – quae mihi scripsisti – meditor in corde meo; ignorant quo spiritu ducantur . . . carentiam caritatis pro zelo accipiunt . . . Verba haec tibi Spiritus dictavit; altam consonantiam inducunt in aure et corde meo. Vere Dominus speciali praedilectione te afficit; vere Dominus habet aliquid quod tibi committat pro gravitate horae nostrae, ut adlaboraveris pro bono fratrum, pro gloria Dei et Christi, pro renovatione animarum in caritate. Te beatum dico et dicam! quod Deus te uti vult ad Sua opera explenda.

Nunc, a te quoddam donum exopto, semper relatum ad horam actualem, quae ruit, et urget: velim ut tu, pro tua in me dilectione, scribere digneris quod cogitas de statu morali nostri temporis, quid tibi videtur de causa et origine difficultatum, de divisione hominum inter se, anxietatibus pro mundi salute . . . etc. quae tibi Dominus inspiraverit. Velim ut remedia salutaria indices, prout tibi opportuna videntur ad mala reparanda et tollenda, ad animos renovandos, ad unitatem cordium in caritate

✠ *88* ✠

25

Most beloved in Christ,

Grace and peace be multiplied to you and yours.

In these days, along with many brothers of this congregation of Poor Servants of the Divine Providence, I have time free for spiritual exercises; for they are exercises for the reformation of morals, for attaining perfection for the renovation of the religious life. In silence and in meditation on the eternal truths, I hear the voice of God which excites our heart to greater love. Pray, dearest brother, that I may not receive the grace of God in vain; but that in fear and joy I receive God's grace and succeed in gaining more grace in addition.

For while directing my thoughts to God and to my soul, I think of you in a very special way in these days of grace and truth; your words especially, the ones you have written to me, I meditate in my heart: "they know not by what Spirit they are led. They take lack of charity for zeal."

These words the Spirit has inspired you with; they brought to my ear and my heart a profound agreement. Truly the Lord has bestowed upon you a special favour; truly the Lord has some-thing which He enjoins on you because of the gravity of our times, that you may labour for the good of the brethren, for the glory of God and Christ, and for the renewal of souls in charity. I call you blessed, and always shall! because God wills to use you in the carrying out of His works.

Now I desire from you a certain gift, always related to the present time which rushes and presses on: I wish that for your love of me, you would see fit to write what you think about the moral state of our times, what your view is about the cause and

provehendam . . . Ut uno verbo dicam: quid de re quae ad Religionem spectat tibi videtur, et quid cogitas faciendum: hoc desidero.

Nimium peto? veniam mihi praebe; est magnae dilectionis ad invicem, est bonitatis tuae erga me, si tantum peto. Ut ex nunc tibi gratias ago.

Providentia divina nos adstringit suavibus vinculis caritatis, etsi de praesentia nunquam nos cognovimus. Sed in caritate, in oratione pro invicem nos cognoscimus bene, optime. In coelo apud Deum nos videbimus, de miseratione Domini, qui redemit nos.

Vale, et etiam pro me ora Deum ut in curriculo vitae gratiam Dei lucri faciam. Ego semper pro to oro ut omne desiderium tuum adimpleatur in pace et prosperitate quae est a Domino.

IN C. J. SAC. J. CALABRIA

origin of our difficulties, about the division of men among themselves, anxieties for the salvation of the world, and other things which the Lord may inspire in you. I would like you to indicate saving remedies, so far as they seem opportune to you for reparation and the removal of evil, for the renewal of courage, for advancing the unity of hearts in charity. To put it in a word, how does it seem to you in regard to Religion, and what do you think needs to be done? That is what I long for.

Do I ask too much? Please forgive me. It belongs to our great love for each other, to your goodness towards me, that I ask so much. As from now, I thank you.

Divine Providence binds us together with the sweet bonds of love, even if we have never known each other personally. But in love and mutual prayer we know each other well, very well. In heaven we shall see each other in the presence of God by the mercy of the Lord who has redeemed us.

Farewell, and also pray to God for me that in the course of my life I may win the grace of God. I always pray for you that your every longing may be fulfilled in peace and in the prosperity which is from the Lord.

In Christ Jesus,

REV. J. CALABRIA

26

Magdalen College
Oxford

XV Sept. MCMLIII

Pater dilectissime,

Gratias ago pro epistola tua, data iii Sept., necnon pro exemplari libri cui nomen *Instaurare Omnia in Christo.*

De statu morali nostri temporis (cum me jusseris garrire) haec sentio. Seniores, ut nos ambo sumus, semper sunt *laudatores temporis acti,* semper cogitant mundum pejorem esse quam fuerit in suis juvenilibus annis. Ergo cavendum est ne fallamur. Hôc tamen proposito, certe sentio gravissima pericula nobis incumbere. Haec eveniunt quia maxima pars Europae apostasiam fecit de fide Christiana. Hinc status pejor quam illum statum quem habuimus ante fidem receptam. Nemo enim ex Christianismo redit in statum quem habuit ante Christianismum, sed in pejorem: tantum distat inter paganum et apostatam quantum innuptam et adulteram. Nam fides perficit naturam sed fides amissa corrumpit naturam. Ergo plerique homines nostri temporis amiserunt non modo lumen supernaturale sed etiam lumen illud naturale quod pagani habuerunt. Sed Deus qui Deus misericordiarum est etiam nunc non omnino demisit genus humanum. In junioribus licet videamus multam crudelitatem et libidinem, nonne simul videmus plurimas virtutum scintillas quibus fortasse nostra generatio caruit. Quantam fortitudinem, quantam curam de pauperibus aspicimus! Non desperandum. Et haud spernendus numerus (apud nos) iam redeunt in fidem.

Haec de statu praesenti: de remediis difficilior quaestio. Equidem credo laborandum esse non modo in evangelizando (hoc certe) sed etiam in quâdam praeparatione evangelica. Necesse est multos ad legem naturalem revocare antequam de

26

Dearest Father,

Thank you for your letter dated 3rd September and also for the copy of the book entitled *The Renewal of All Things in Christ*.

Regarding the moral condition of our times (since you bid me prattle on) I think this. Older people, as we both are, are always "praisers of times past". They always think the world is worse than it was in their young days. Therefore we ought to take care lest we go wrong. But, with this proviso, certainly I feel that very grave dangers hang over us. This results from the apostasy of the great part of Europe from the Christian faith. Hence a worse state than the one we were in before we received the Faith. For no one returns from Christianity to the same state he was in before Christianity but into a worse state: the difference between a pagan and an apostate is the difference between an unmarried woman and an adulteress. For faith perfects nature but faith lost corrupts nature. Therefore many men of our time have lost not only the supernatural light but also the natural light which pagans possessed.

But God, who is the God of mercies, even now has not altogether cast off the human race. In younger people, although we may see much cruelty and lust, yet at the same time do we not see very many sparks of virtues which perhaps our own generation lacked? How much courage, how much concern for the poor do we see! We must not despair. And (among us) a not inconsiderable number are now returning to the Faith.

So much for the present situation. About remedies the question is more difficult. For my part I believe we ought to work not

Deo loquamur. Christus enim promittit remissionem peccatorum: sed quid hoc ad eos qui, quum legem naturalem ignorent, nesciunt se peccavisse. Quis medicamentum accipiet nisi se morbo teneri sciat? Relativismus moralis hostis est quem debemus vincere antequam Atheismum aggrediamur. Fere auserim dicere "Primo faciamus juniores bonos Paganos et postea faciamus Christianos". Deliramenta haec? Sed habes quod petisti. Semper et tu et congregatio tua in orationibus meis. Vale,

C. S. LEWIS

[Don Giovanni Calabria died
on 4th December 1954]

27

Magdalen College
Oxford

Dec. 5° 1954

Heus, pater dilectissime, quantum inter nos silentium! Magnopere mihi cordi erit si iterum de te et rebus tuis rescripseris. Mihi quidem mox migrandum est ex Oxonia in Cantabrigiam in quâ universitate electus sum Professor Anglarum Literarum Medii

only at spreading the Gospel (that certainly) but also at a certain preparation for the Gospel. It is necessary to recall many to the law of nature *before* we talk about God. For Christ promises forgiveness of sins: but what is that to those who, since they do not know the law of nature, do not know that they have sinned? Who will take medicine unless he knows he is in the grip of disease? Moral relativity is the enemy we have to overcome before we tackle Atheism. I would almost dare to say "First let us make the younger generation good pagans and afterwards let us make them Christians".

These are ravings? But you have what you requested.

Always you and your Congregation are in my prayers.

Farewell,

C. S. LEWIS

[Don Giovanni Calabria died
on 4th December 1954]

27

Magdalen College
Oxford

5th December 1954

Good Heavens, dearest Father, what a long silence there has been between us!

It will be a great delight to me if you write back to me again about yourself and your affairs.

Aevi et Renascentiae. Coelestem patronam tamen non mutabo, nam apud Cantabrigienses adscribor Collegio Stae. M. Magdalenae. Orthographiâ vero discrepant (Oxonienses Magdalen, Cantabrigienses vero Magdalene scribunt) sed idem sonant, i.e. *Modlin*. Fides Christiana, ut puto, magis valet apud Cantabrigienses quam apud nostros; communistae rariores sunt et pestiferi philosophi quos logicales positivistos vocamus haud aeque pollunt.

Sed to quid agis? Valesne adhuc? Scito saltem me semper pro te orare, et nunc praesertim dum nos paramus ad suavissimum festum Sanctae Nativitatis. Congaudeamus, mi pater, quamvis loco divisi, spiritu tamen et caritatê uniti, et ora semper pro

C. S. LEWIS

As for me, I have soon to migrate from Oxford to Cambridge at which University I have been elected Professor of Mediaeval and Renaissance English Literature.

However, I shall not change my heavenly Patroness because at Cambridge I shall be a member of the College of St Mary Magdalene. In spelling they indeed differ (Oxford writes Magdalen, Cambridge on the other hand Magdalene) but they are pronounced the same, i.e. Modlin.

The Christian Faith, as I think, counts for more among Cambridge men than among us; Communists are rarer and those plaguey philosophers whom we call Logical Positivists do not polute as much.

But what are you doing? Are you still in good health?

Know at least that I always pray for you, and especially at this time when we are preparing for that dearest of festivals, the Feast of the Holy Nativity.

Let us rejoice together, my Father: though divided in space, yet in spirit and charity we are united: and may you ever pray for

C. S. LEWIS

THE LATIN LETTERS
BETWEEN
C. S. LEWIS
and
DON LUIGI PEDROLLO
(1954–1961)

After the death of Don Giovanni Calabria, C. S. Lewis
continued the correspondence with Don Luigi Pedrollo,
a distinguished member of the Verona congregation.

28

Magdalen College
Oxford

Dec. xvi MCMLIV

Reverende Pater,

Doleo et vobis condoleo de obitu dilectissimi amici. Ille quidem ex aerumnis hujus saeculi, quas gravissime sentire solebat in patriam feliciter migravit; vobis procul dubio acerbus luctus. Gratias ago pro photographia quam mittendo bene fecisti. Aspectus viri taus est qualem auguratus sum; senilis gravitas bene mixta et composita cum quadum juvenili alacritate. Semper et ipsius et congregationis vestrae memoriam in orationes habebo; et vos idem pro me facturos spero.

Vale,

C. S. LEWIS

28

Magdalen College
Oxford

16th December 1954

Reverend Father,

I grieve and condole with you at the death of a most dearly loved friend. He, indeed, from the troubles of this world which he used to feel most heavily, has happily passed over into his own Country; to you without doubt the grief is keen.

I thank you for the photograph which it was good of you to send me. His appearance is such as I had imagined: the gravity of age well mixed and combined with a certain youthful vivacity. I shall always make remembrance of him and of your Congregation in my prayers and I hope that you will do the same for me.

Farewell,

C. S. LEWIS

29

Magdalene College

Cambridge

Jan. 19 1959

Bene fecisti, reverende pater, mittendo mihi pulcherrimum librum de carissimi Patris Joanni vita. Gratias ago. Spero me ex lectione hujus libri certiorem fieri de multis quae adhuc latebant; saepe enim vir me sanctus in suis epistolis insinuabat se nescioquo secreto dolore laborare, occultis Dei consiliis qui flagellat omnem filium quem accipit.

Feliciter evenit ad te ut scribam hac hebdomade quo omnes qui profitentur fidem Christi tenentur orationes facere pro redintegratione Ecclesiae nunc, eheu, laceratae et divisae.

Vale,

C. S. LEWIS

30

Collegium Stae Mariae Magdalenae apud

Cantabrigienses

xxviii Mart. 1959

Reverendissime Pater,

Grato animo te tuosque [saluto] hoc die solemni et severo quo Dominus noster animabus incarceratis praedicavit salutem. Ego meique valemus. Nunc scribo libellum *De IV Amoribus i.e.* Graece

29

Magdalene College
Cambridge

19th January 1959

It was good of you, reverend Father, to send me this most beautiful book about the life of dearest Father John. I thank you. I hope that from reading this book I shall become better informed about many things which till now have remained obscure; for often this holy man in his letters implied that he laboured under I know not what secret grief, in the hidden counsels of God who chastises everyone whom He receives as a son.

Happily it occurs that I write to you in this Week when all who profess themselves Christians are bound to offer prayers for the reunion of the Church, now, alas, torn and divided. Farewell.

C. S. LEWIS

30

The College of St Mary Magdalene
Cambridge

Easter Saturday 28th March 1959

Most Reverend Father,

With a grateful heart I salute you and yours on this solemn and serious day on which the Lord preached to the souls in prison. I and mine are well.

Storgé, Philia, Eros, Agapé – quibus vocabulis utor quia Latina nomina desunt. Ora pro me Ut Deus mihi concedat aut salutaria aut saltem haud nocitura dicere. Nam "periculosae plenum opus aleae" ut Flaccus scripsit. Casa vestra semper in orationibus meis. Valete in Salvatore nostro.

C. S. LEWIS

31

E Collegio Stae Mariae Magdalenae
apud Cantabrigienses

xv Dec. mcmlix

Reverende Pater,

Gratias cordialiter ago pro benevolis tuis litteris. Scito domum vestram quotidie in orationibus meis nominari. Et tu orationibus pro nobis insta. Nunc enim, post biennium remissionis redit uxoris meae letalis morbus. Placeat Domino, ut quodcunque de corpore voluerit, integri maneant animi amborum; ut fides intacta nos corroboret, contritio emolliat, pax laetificet. Et hoc usque ad nunc fit; neque faciliter crederes quanta gaudia inter medias aerumnas nonnumquam sentiamus. Quid mirum? Nonne consolationem lugentibus pollicitus est? Vale.

C. S. LEWIS

Now I am writing a little book on *The Four Loves*, i.e., in *Storgé*, *Philia*, *Eros*, and *Agapé* – I use these words because there are no names for them in Latin.

Pray for me that God grant me to say things helpful to salvation, or at least not harmful. For this is a work "full of dangerous hazard" as Flaccus wrote.

Your House is ever in my prayers,

Farewell in our Saviour,

C. S. LEWIS

31

The College of St Mary Magdalene
Cambridge

15th December 1959

Reverend Father,

I send you my cordial thanks for your kind letter.

Be assured that your House is daily named in my prayers. And do you persevere in prayers for us. For now, after two years' remission, my wife's mortal illness has returned. May it please the Lord that, whatever is His will for the body, the minds of both of us may remain unharmed; that faith unimpaired may strengthen us, contrition soften us and peace make us joyful.

And that, up till now, has happened; nor would you readily believe what joys we sometimes experience in the midst of troubles. What wonder? For has He not promised comfort to those who mourn?

Farewell,

C. S. LEWIS

32

quasi e Collegio Stae Mariae
Magdalenae apud
Cantabrigienses

Pascha 1960

Reverende Pater,

Gratias ago pro benevolis litteris vestris. Gaudeo me locum adhuc tenere in memoria vestra; et vos et vestri quotidie in orationibus estis. Equidem hoc tempore in magnâ aerumnâ sum. Nihilominus sursum corda: Christus enim resurrexit. Vale.

C. S. LEWIS

33

Collegium Stae Mariae Magdalenensis
apud Cantabrigienses
Anglia

iii Jan. MCMLXI

Gratias tibi ago, mi pater, pro amicabili epistola et te tuosque in his beatissimis festis saluto.

Vellem me posse ad te mittere exemplaria epistolarum quas scripsit Ven. Pater D. Ioannes Calabria. Sed neque ipsas epistolas

32

as from The College of St Mary Magdalene
Cambridge

Easter 1960
16th April 1960

Reverend Father,

I thank you for your kind letter. I rejoice that I still hold a place in your memory; both you and yours are daily in my prayers.

As for me, I am at this time in great trouble.

None the less, let us lift up our hearts: for Christ is risen. Farewell,

C. S. LEWIS

33

The College of St Mary Magdalene
Cambridge
England

3rd January 1961

I thank you, my Father, for your friendly letter, and I greet you and yours on this most blessed festival.

I wish I could send you copies of the letters which the Venerable Father Don John Calabria wrote. But I have neither the

neque exemplaria habeo. Moris est mei omnes epistolas post biduum ignibus dare. Non, mi crede, quia nullo pretio Illas aestimo; immo quia res saepe sacro dignas silentio posteris legendas relinquere nolo. Nunc enim curiosi scrutatores omnia nostra effodiunt et veneno publicitatis (ut rem barbaram verbo barbaro nominem) aspergunt. Quod fieri minime vellem de Patris Joannis epistolis. Admirabilis ille vir aliis mitissimus idemque sibi severissimus vel saevissimus, humilitate et quadam sancta imprudentiâ multa scripsit quae tacenda puto. Hanc meam apologiam velim curialibus verbis Patri Mondrone patefacias.

Multo gaudemus de recenti colloquio inter Sanctum Patrem et nostrum Archiepiscopum. Dominus corroboret bonum omen.

Uxor mea mense Jul. mortem obiit. Pro illa et me orationes reduplica. Tu et domus tua semper in meis sunt. Vale.

C. S. LEWIS

letters themselves nor copies of them. It is my practice to consign to the flames all letters after two days – not, believe me, because I esteem them of no value, rather because I do not wish to relinquish things often worthy of sacred silence to subsequent reading by posterity.

For nowadays inquisitive researchers dig out all our affairs and besmirch them with the poison of "publicity" (as a barbarous thing I am giving it a barbarous name).

This is the last thing I would wish to happen to the letters of Father John.

That admirable man, to others most lenient but to himself most severe, not to say savage, out of humility and with a certain holy imprudence wrote many things which I think should be kept quiet. If you would politely convey this explanation of mine to Father Mondrone, I would be grateful.

We greatly rejoice at the recent meeting between the Holy Father and our Archbishop. May the Lord confirm this happy omen.

My wife died in the month of July. For her and for me redouble your prayers. You and your House are ever in mine.

Farewell,

C. S. LEWIS

34

The College of St Mary Magdalene
Cambridge

8th April in the year of our Salvation 1961

Dear Father,

I was glad to receive your letter. The Feast Days for my part, alas, I spent in bed suffering from a fever; now I am somewhat restored to health, God be thanked. I return your greetings and I offer prayers for you and your House.

I know that you pour forth your prayers both for my most dearly-longed-for wife and also for me who – now bereaved and as it were halved – journey on, through this Vale of Tears, alone.

Farewell,

C. S. LEWIS

34

Collegium Stae Mariae Magdalenae
apud Cantabrigienses

viii Apr. MCMLXI salv. Nostrae

Dilecte Pater,

Grato animo accepi litteras vestras. Dies festos, eheu, equidem in lectulo degi, febre laborans; nunc admodum sanatus, Deo
gratias, salutationes vestras reddo et vota pro vobis et domo vestra facio. Scio vos preces effundere et pro desideratissima uxore
mea et pro me qui jam orbatus et quasi dimidiatus solus hanc
vallem lacrimarum peragro. Valete,

C. S. LEWIS

NOTES ON THE LETTERS

LETTER 1 (01.09.47)

This is the opening letter of the correspondence, the first from Don Giovanni Calabria to C. S. Lewis. Don Calabria made it part of his mission to enter into correspondence with members of other Churches. Some account of this is given by Clara Sarrocco, in a perceptive article in *The Bulletin of the C. S. Lewis Society,* New York, February 1987. Don Calabria's addressees included the Archbishop of Canterbury (in 1949) and representatives of the Orthodox and Lutheran communions, in particular Pastor Suni Wiman of Sweden. Don Giovanni's letters to Lewis as still extant (*i.e.* letters of which Verona holds copies) are frequently general in scope but are diversified here and there by specific personal references. One of the letters exists only in draft Italian; and Don Giovanni may have drawn upon local academic help in translating into Latin his more general passages, passages he may have sent to more than one recipient. In the typed copies the Latin is sometimes corrupt, if not inexact. The correspondence itself proceeds at intervals of several months and indeed longer. But at times it goes back and forth by near return of post. For example, having written to Lewis his letter of 1st September 1947, and then having had Lewis's reply of 6th September, Don Calabria evidently wrote again on 15th September but of that letter the text is no longer found.

One of the houses: Don Giovanni acquired a tenth-century Abbey, originally Benedictine, and now called La Casa di Maguzzano, near Lake Garda (Sarrocco, *loc cit).*

an octave: the January octave for unity is something Don Calabria reverts to from time to time and it was close to his heart.

Le Lettere di Berlicche: the Italian title of *The Screwtape Letters.* Published by Arnaldo Mondadori. It was brought to Don Calabria's notice by Father Genovesi OP.

LETTER 2 (06.09.47)
This is C. S. Lewis's first letter to Don Giovanni Calabria and its emphasis on prayer – "what is most efficacious", prayer – sets a keynote for the rest of the correspondence.

LETTER 3 (20.09.47)
Common perils: In a letter of 8th May 1939 *(Letters of C. S. Lewis,* edited by W. H. Lewis, Bles 1966) Lewis expressed to Dom Bede Griffiths somewhat similar thoughts. "A united Christendom should be the answer to the new Paganism. But how reconciliation of the Churches as opposed to conversion of individuals from one Church to another is to come about I confess I cannot see. I am inclined to think that the immediate task is vigorous cooperation on the basis of what even now is common – combined of course with full admission of the differences. An experienced unity on some things ought then prove the prelude to a confessional unity on all things. Nothing could give such strong support to the Papal claims as the spectacle of a Pope actually functioning as the head of Christendom."

LETTER 4 (03.10.47)
thy face: Genesis 3:19.

LETTER 5 (25.11.47)
do miracles in some place. See Mark 6:5.

tota opera . . . perlegi: I have read all (their) works right through. An example of Lewis's massive – and characteristic – thoroughness and, be it added, fairness. Doubtless he read these

works in preparing his volume for *The Oxford History of English Literature* (OHEL). See note below on Letter 7.

my own words: The Vulgate reads *"si quis voluerit voluntatem ejus facere, cognoscet de doctrina"* (John 7:17) which Bishop Challoner's Douay version translates "if any man will do the will of him (his will A.V.) he shall know of the doctrine".

France: the fall of the French Government in August had precipitated a crisis which was still unresolved.

LETTER 6 (13.01.48 or 13.06.48)

"Sine vicissitudinis umbra" is no doubt an echo of James 1:17: neither shadow of turning (A.V.); *nec vicistitudinis odumbratio* (Vulgate).

Dr. Lodetti of Verona: The correspondence gives no further light on who he was.

Verona date this letter "Jun." not "Jan." My own first reading of the MS was "Jan.". This could well prove wrong but I have left the letter as Jan., pending further evidence, because the references to the Octave of Unity and to other contacts with Verona (Dr Lodetti) seem to fit the context. See also the dating of 14.01.53.

LETTER 7 (27.03.48)

hora novissima: from the poem of Bernard of Morlaix (c. 1130).

Lewis's translation of Dunbar (1460-1522) echoes Catullus Carmina V *"unius aestimemus assis"*, see Book I, Chapter I, "The Close of the Middle Ages in Scotland", in Lewis's volume in *The Oxford History of English Literature* (OHEL), ed. F. P. Wilson and Bonamy Dobrée, namely the volume entitled *English Literature in the Sixteenth Century excluding Drama*. This was the completion of The Clark Lectures at Trinity College, Cambridge, in 1944 and it was published, in 1954, by the OUP. The couplet (see page 97) runs as follows:

> Man pleis [i.e. please] thy Makar and be mirry
> And sett nocht by this world a chirry.

Sursum corda: from the Liturgy: lift up your hearts. Followed immediately by that line from the *Aeneid* (I.203) where Aeneas encourages his comrades with the thought that hardships endured may, some day, be a joy to recall. So, Lewis implies, may the tribulations of this life be in the life to come.

LETTER 8 (10.08.48)

beareth all things: fert omnia, credit omnia: 1 Corinthians 13:7 Vulgate *omnia suffert.*

no temptation: 1 Corinthians 10:3: *tentatio vos non apprehendit nisi humana* (Vulgate).

not yet unto blood, etc. *Nondum enim usque ad sanguinem restitistis:* you have not yet resisted unto blood. Ep. Hebr. 12:4

Matthew 7:15: *in vestimentis ovium.*

James 1:3: *Scientes quod probatio fidei vestrae patientiam operatur.*

LETTER 9 (14.01.49)

tents of Kedar: Psalm 120:5 (Vulgate CXIX). Lewis's "aged mother" was the lady whom Lewis, until her death in 1951, took care of as if she were his own mother when her son, Lewis's close friend, Paddy Moore, was killed in France (1918) in World War 1.

LETTER 10 (17.04.49)

Dictavi: composed, or dictated: perhaps Don Calabria did sometimes dictate – and then add a few lines in manuscript on the back of the typescript.

LETTER 11 (10.09.49)

Accidia (Greek: akedia) sloth; not caring, indifference or torpor from grief or exhaustion: one of the Seven Deadly Sins.

your poet: Dante. *Inferno* 3, 18.

rumours of wars: Mark 13:7 *cum audieritis autem belly et opiniones bellorum ne timueritis* (Vulgate).

Vester: your, in the plural: yours, i.e., as to you and to your House too.

LETTER 12 (18.09.49)

glorify the Father: Matthew 5:16, *ut videant opera vestra bona et glorificent patrem vestrum qui in coelis est.*

our sufficiency is of God: 2 Corinthians 3:5.

can do all things: Philippians 4:13, *omnia possum in eo qui me confortat.*

LETTER 13 (19.11.49)

a Sibylline book: i.e. a mysteriously unintelligible one.

1. Matthew 18:3 *nisi conversi fueritis et efficiamini sicut parvuli, non intrabitis in regnum coelorum.*

received today (19.11.49): there is an entry in the Verona archives which records a letter sent to Lewis on 12.11.49: *"Lettera di Don Paolo Arnaboldi inviata al Prof. Lewis su consiglio di Don Giovanni Calabria, 12.11.49."*

LETTER 14 (17.12.49)

dwell together in unity: Psalm 132:1 (Vulgate) (131 BCP).

Philippians 4:7: *Et pax Dei qui exsuperet omnem sensum custodiat corda vestra a intellegentias vestras in Christo Jesu* (Vulgate).

And the peace of God which surpasseth all understanding keep your hearts and minds in Christ Jesus (Challoner).

LETTER 15 (13.09.51)

my tale: presumably one of his stories for children.

LETTER 16 (26.12.51)

Colossians 2:14: *Delens quod adversus nos erat chirographiam decreti* (Vulgate). Blotting out the handwriting of the decree that was against us (Challoner).

Hebrews 11:1: *Est autem fides sperandarum substantia rerum* (Vulgate). Now faith is the substance of things to be hoped for (Douay).

Psalm 8:2; Matthew 21;16: *Ex ore infantium,* out of the mouths of infants, *etc.*

Numbers 22:28.

Philippians 4:4: *Gaudete in Domino semper: iterum dico gaudete.* Rejoice in the Lord alway: and again I say, Rejoice.

LETTER 17 (14.4.52)

venio, I come. Compare *Veni, Domine Jesus,* "come Lord Jesus", Revelation/Apocalypse 22,20. C. S. Lewis's confessor was Father Walter Adams of The Society of St John The Evangelist (SSJE). He was born in 1871 and died at the Altar on 3rd March 1952. (For this information I am indebted to Father Walter Hooper.)

Amor, etc. Love is a fire continuously burning. Source is the *Imitatio* (bk. 4 cap. 4).

that they all may be one: John 17:21: *ut omnes unum sint.*

LETTER 18 (14.07.52)

Romans 13:11: *nunc enim propior est salus quam cum credidimus. Dies illa.* Matthew 24:36: *De die autem illa . . . nemo scit.*

(Compare also the *Dies Irae, dies illa* by Thomas of Celano c. AD 1255).

St John: St John The Divine. This allusion to the Apocalypse conflates the AV. "Surely I come quickly, Amen. Even so, come, Lord Jesus", and the Vulgate *"Etiam venio cito; Amen. Veni, Domine Jesu* (Revelation/Apocalypse XXII, 20).

that supreme command: John 13:34: *Mandatum novum do vobis, Ut diligatis invicem sicut dilexi vos.*

that peace which no one can take from us: John 16:22: *et gaudium vestrum nemo tollet a vobis.* John 14:27: *Pacem relinquo vobis, pacem meam; do vobis.* Compare Luke 10:42: *Maria optimam partem elegit quae non auferetur ab ea.*

our redemption is now nearer: Luke 21:28: *Levate capita vestra quoniam appropinquat redemptio vestra.*

LETTER 19 (05.01.53)

The book on Prayer might be his posthumously published *Letters to Malcolm*. But he had probably worked on the earlier version at an earlier date.

the Ark: 1 Chronicles XIII, 9: *tetendit Oza manum suam ut sustentaret arcam . . . at mortuus est ibi coram Domino.*

the plough: Luke 9:62: *nemo mittens manum suam ad aratrum, at respiciens retro, aptus est regno Dei.*

LETTER 20 (07.01.53)

The article *"Responsabilità"* by Father Manna (signed S. P. Manna) appeared in the 1952 October issue of the magazine *Amico*. In it, the author pleads for greater recognition of the gravity of current Communist persecution of Christians (hospital workers no less than missionaries) in China. If a Communist *(e.g.* Jacques Declos) is arrested in the West, the Communist world rises to protest. There should be at least no less an outcry on behalf of victimized missionaries.

In his reply Lewis mentions having himself received letters on the subject. From 1927 to 1931 his brother, Major Warren Lewis, had served in Army postings in China (Kowloon and Shanghai). Lewis does not mention this but it may lie behind his reference to "our" prayers for suffering China.

LETTER 21 (09.01.53)

This letter exists only in pencilled manuscript in Italian, and the text here given is that of the typed Verona transcript.

LETTER 22 (14.01.53)

The date here given (14th January) again conjectures that Lewis's manuscript abbreviation of the month is for January, not June, and this is confirmed by Lewis's acknowledging the letter of 9th January.

The problem of petitionary prayer was one Lewis was later to put to the Oxford Clerical Society in a paper on 8th December 1953 (Petitionary Prayer: a problem without an answer). It would have been interesting to have had Don Calabria's reply if one was sent.

if it be possible: Matthew 26:39; Mark 14:35.

LETTER 23 (17.03.53)

the Just one: see *e.g.* Acts 7:52.

LETTER 24 (10.08.53)

know not by what Spirit they are led: Luke 9:55: what manner of Spirit you are of (AV). *Nescitis cujus spiritus estis* (Vulgate).

covers a multitude of sins: 1 Peter 4:8.

suis: so the MS; not *nostris.* Supply *quisque* after *suis.*

LETTER 25 (03.09.53)

gaining: *superlucrari* : to gain in addition. Compare the parable of the talents: *ecce alia quinque superlucratus sum* (Vulgate); behold I have gained other five over and above. Matthew 25:20.

LETTER 26 (15.09.53)

The need to preserve or restore human nature as being nowadays under threat forms a central theme of Lewis' book, *The Abolition of Man.*

For *"temporis acti"* see Horace, *Ars Poetica 173-4: Difficilis, querulus, laudator temporis acti/Se puero.* (Testy, a grumbler inclined to praise the way the world went when he was a boy.)

LETTER 27 (05.12.54)

Unknown to Lewis, this letter was written one day after Don Calabria's death. He died in Verona on 4th December 1954.

LETTER 28 (16.12.54)

This letter or part of a letter is also found in Italian (see The

Lateran thesis, *Il Servo di Dio* by Eugenio Dal Corso). Evidently the Congregation at Verona informed Lewis of their Founder's death some time after the receipt of his letter of 5th December 1954. In doing so, they included a photograph of Don Calabria and thereby elicited this acknowledgement from Lewis.

LETTER 29 (19.01.59)

The first edition of the biography of Don Giovanni, *"Don Giovanni Calabria, Servo di Dio"* (Otto Foffano) was prefaced by Sac. Luigi Pedrolla at Verona on 15th October 1953. There is nothing in C. S. Lewis's letter to Verona of 6th January 1961 to show that for him what were obscurities had by then been resolved. In corroboration there are, however, a few passages which tell of times of anguish and inadequacy *(loc. cit.* pp. 308, 309 and 313) when faith seemed lost, nothing good done and prayer – except for expiation – seemingly impossible.

After an illness of much suffering Don Calabria died peacefully, one of his last acts being to give his blessing to his doctor (and to his doctor's family, to the third and fourth generations). See also *"Il servo di Dio, Don Giovanni Calabria"* by Fra Elviro Dall'Ora (Verona, 1979) and *"Ricordo di Don Luigi Pedrollo, primo successors di Don Calabria"* (Verona, 1987).

LETTER 30 (28.03.59)

Preached to the souls in prison: 1 Peter 3:19.

The Four Loves was published in 1960 (the four being affection, friendship, Eros and charity). For an interesting comment on this book see the reference to it by Lewis's fellow-Inkling, Owen Barfield, in his Introduction to *The Meaning of Love* by Vladimir Solovyov, translated by Jane Marshall (as substantially revised by Thomas R. Beyer Jr.) and published in the Floris Classics by The Centenary Press 1945 and Floris Books (Billings and Sons, Worcester) 1984. In the U.S.A., the Lindisfarne Press.

Flaccus: Horace. See Odes 2.1.6. In this Ode, Horace warns his

friend Pollio that in writing the history of critical events in which he, Pollio, was involved, he was undertaking a work "full of dangerous hazard", *"periculosae plenum opus aleae"*.

LETTER 31 (15.12.59)

From now on Lewis's letters are increasingly grave, though never without faith and the expression of faith. How after the laying on of hands, 21st March 1957, Joy, his wife, experienced relief and recovery from cancer; how, after an interval of some three years, the cancer nevertheless returned and finally proved fatal has been told elsewhere. From this letter it would appear that in some earlier letter not yet traced or no longer extant Lewis must have told the Fathers at Verona of Joy's illness and amazing recovery. Now he tells them of the cancer's return. Courageously he adds that even in grief he and his wife experience joys and the truth of the beatitude, *beati qui lugent quoniam ipsi consolabuntur* (Matthew 5:5): Blessed are they who mourn for they shall be comforted.

integri animi. The MS has *integres.* Perhaps Lewis intended *integrae . . . animae,* meaning "may our *souls* remain unharmed".

LETTER 32 (16.4.60)

The note of grief continues. But even so – as in the Liturgy and now because of Easter, *sursum corda,* let us lift up our hearts (literally, "your hearts"; with the reply, "we lift them up unto the Lord").

LETTER 33 (03.01.61)

curialibus verbis: in my original Summary I had equated this phrase with "officially" and I am indebted to Sir David Hunt for pointing out that it clearly means "with courteous words", "politely". The Verona fathers on receiving it read it similarly, i.e. in language befitting a message addressed to an ecclesiastic. Mr Colin Hardie comments that Lewis would frequently have met

this sense of courteous and courtesy in Dante's *de Vulgari Eloquentia.*

LETTER 34 (08.04.61)

Bereaved and "as it were halved", Lewis journeys on alone. He died at Oxford, a week before his sixty-fifth birthday, on 22nd November 1963 (see *C. S. Lewis: a Biography* by Roger Lancelyn Green and Walter Hooper; Collins, 1964).

INDEX OF LETTERS

11. From C. S. Lewis   Oxford
    Dilecte Pater, Nuper in scriniis   10th September 1949

12. From Don Calabria   Verona
    Dilectissime in Domino   18th September 1949

    (Letter in Italian, from Don Paolo   12th November 1949
    Arnaboldi to C. S. Lewis, in a
    manuscript which Lewis could
    not decipher)

13. From C. S. Lewis   Oxford
    Dilectissime Pater, Remitto   19th November 1949

14. From Don Calabria   Verona
    Dilectissime in Christo, Gratia tibi   17th December 1949

15. From C. S. Lewis   Oxford
    Dilectissime Pater, Insolito gaudio   13th September 1951

16. From C. S. Lewis   Oxford
    Dilectissime Pater, Grato animo   26th December 1951

17. From C. S. Lewis   Oxford
    Pater dilectissime, Multum eras   14th April 1952

18. From C. S. Lewis   Oxford
    Gratias ago, dilectissime pater   14th July 1952

19. From C. S. Lewis   Oxford
    Dilectissime Pater, Grato animo   5th January 1953

20. From C. S. Lewis   Oxford
    Tandem, pater dilectissime   7th January 1953

21. From Don Calabria   Verona
    Siamo in giorni santi   (?) 9th January 1953

22. From C. S. Lewis   Oxford
    Pater dilectissime, Multo gaudio   14th January (?June)
                                           1953

23. From C. S. Lewis   Oxford
    Dilectissime Pater, Gavisus sum   17th March 1953

24. From C. S. Lewis   Oxford
    Dilectissime Pater, Accepi   10th August 1953

25. From Don Calabria   Verona
    Dilectissime in Christo, Gratia et pax   3rd September 1953

26. From C. S. Lewis   Oxford
    Pater dilectissime, Gratias ago   15th September 1953

27. From C. S. Lewis   Oxford
    Heus, pater dilectissime   5th December 1954

Death of Don Giovanni Calabria in Verona on 4th
December 1954. Later the Fathers there inform C. S.
Lewis and send him a photograph of Don Calabria.
Henceforth Lewis's correspondent is Don Luigi
Pedrollo.

28. From C. S. Lewis   Oxford
    Reverende Pater, Doleo   16th December 1954

29. From C. S. Lewis   Cambridge
    Bene fecisti   19th January 1959

30. From C. S. Lewis   Cambridge
    Reverendissime Pater, Grato animo   28th March 1959

31. From C. S. Lewis   Cambridge
    Reverende Pater, Gratias cordialiter   15th December 1959

32. From C. S. Lewis   Cambridge
    Reverende Pater, Gratias ago   16th April 1960

33. From C. S. Lewis   Cambridge
    Gratias tibi ago   3rd January 1961

34 From C. S. Lewis   Cambridge
    Dilecte Pater, Grato animo   8th April, in the year
                                              year of our Salvation
                                              1961